PASSPORT TO AROMATHERAPY

Dr. Joel D. Wallach, BS, DVM, ND
and Dr. Ma Lan, MD, MS, LAC

with

Alexandria Brighton, MF, MA, MB, NAHA
and Dr. Judy Wright, ND, MH, MA, CNHP

Library of Congress Cataloging in Publications Data:

1. Aromatherapy
2. History of aromatherapy
3. Essential Oils
4. Essential Oil chemistry
5. Essential Oil safety
6. Essential Oil blending
7. Essential Oil harvesting & preparation
8. Essential Oil quality control
9. Essential Oil *Materia Medica*

PASSPORT TO AROMATHERAPY
First Edition, September 2005

ISBN No: *0-9748581-2-9*

Printed and published by Wellness Publications LLC
P.O. Box 1222, Bonita, CA 91908
www.drjwallach.com
www.webndtherapy.com

1-800-755-4656 USA and Canada
1-619-420-2435 local and international

Contents

Acknowledgements

Cover Design

We gratefully acknowledge Alexandria Brighton, Jacque Dreher, Bev Day, Vince Marasigan and Jimbo Hamoy for the cover design for *Passport to Aromatherapy* and Ma Hansen for the Chinese graphics and characters.

About the Authors

Dr. Joel Wallach, BS, DVM, ND

Dr. Wallach has been involved in biomedical research and clinical medicine for more than 47 years. He received his BS degree (agriculture) from the University of Missouri with a major in animal husbandry (nutrition) and a minor in field crops and soils; a DVM (veterinary medicine) from the University of Missouri; a three year post doctoral fellowship (comparative pathology/medicine), Washington University, St. Louis, Missouri - The Center for the Biology of Natural Systems (The St. Louis Zoological Gardens, Shaw's Botanical Gardens, Botany Department, Washington University), Iowa State University, Ames, Iowa; Natal Parks Board, Umfolozi and Hluhluwe Game Parks, Republic of South Africa; St. Louis Zoological Gardens; The Chicago Zoological Gardens (Brookfield Zoo); Shedd Aquarium, Chicago, Il; Yerkes Regional Primate Research Center, Emory University, Atlanta, GA; ND (naturopathic physician), the National College of Naturopathic Medicine, Portland, OR; Harbin Medical University, Harbin, Hei Long Jiang and the Shanghai Medical University, People's Republic of China.

He was a member of NIH site visit teams for facilities using exotic animal models for the study of human disease for four years and was a member of the 1968 National Science Foundation ad hoc committee that authored the 1968 Animal Welfare Act (humane housing, nutrition and care of laboratory and captive exotic species); a professor of nutrition at the National College of Naturopathic Medicine, Portland, OR; a Consulting Professor of Medicine, Harbin Medical University, Harbin, Hei Long Jiang, People's Republic of China.

Dr. Wallach has appeared as an expert witness in State and Federal Courts as a comparative pathologist.

Dr. Wallach attained the rank of lieutenant Colonel in the Missouri Air National Guard (131st Tactical Hospital), known as "Lindberg's own," and the Alaskan Air Reserves with responsibilities in public health and prevention and clean up of nuclear, biological and chemical attacks in North America and Europe.

Dr. Wallach was a recipient of the 1991 Wooster Beach Gold Medal Award (Association of Eclectic Physicians) for a significant breakthrough in the basic understanding of the cause and pathophysiology of Cystic Fibrosis. Dr. Wallach was nominated for the 1991 Nobel Prize in Medicine (Association of Eclectic Physicians) for his work in the understanding of the genesis and the pathophysiology of Cystic Fibrosis and other birth defects produced by nutritional deficiencies of the embryo during pregnancy.

Dr. Wallach received the 2004 Guardian of the Constitution Award (Emord & Assoc.) for his proactive and successful litigation efforts in obtaining nutrition claims from the FDA for Selenium and Omega 3 essential fatty acids. He also received the 2004 James Lind Scientific Achievement Award (Emord & Assoc.) for "brilliant discoveries that have paved the way for greater health and longevity" for Americans.

Dr. Wallach has appeared frequently on local and national network and public radio and television (including a special on Cystic Fibrosis with ABC's 20/20), regional and national talk radio programs as an expert on trace mineral and rare earth deficiency diseases. Dr. Wallach is the host of his own syndicated talk radio show programs (Let's Play Doctor and Dead Doctors Don't Lie). Because of his free-wheeling style of humor and ability to zero in on the basic truth in health problems and medical politics he is widely known as the "Rush Limbaugh" of alternative health.

Dr. Wallach has given an average of 300 free health lectures per year for more than 15 years, literally reaching millions of enthusiastic fans. His tape, Dead Doctors Don't Lie (translated into eight languages) has sold more than 62 million copies world wide and has been translated into eight languages. Dr. Wallach has more than 70 peer review publications to his credit including a major reference, The Diseases of Exotic Animals - published by W. B. Saunders. This 1,000 page illustrated text is listed by the Smithsonian Institute as, "A recommended reference for all professional zoological parks and Aquariums."

Dr. Ma Lan, MD, MS, LAc

Dr. Ma Lan was educated in the People's Republic of China. Dr. Ma Lan received her MD (medical degree) from the Beijing Medical University; took her residency at the People's Hospital, Beijing and was a staff surgeon at the Canton Air Force Hospital; she received her MS (master of science) in transplantation immunology from Zhongshan Medical University, Canton, People's Republic of China; as with all Chinese doctors, Dr. Ma Lan was trained in Traditional Chinese Medicine (i.e.- acupuncture, herbs, essential oils, manipulation, food as medicine, massage and hydrotherapy) prior to entering the Western-style medical schools.

Dr. Ma Lan's research credits include being an exchange scholar at the Harvard School of Medicine, Boston, MA; a research fellow in laser microsurgery at St. Joseph Hospital, Houston, TX; the Department of Orthopedic Surgery, the Medical College of Wisconsin, Milwaukee, WI; and the Department of Pharmacology, University of California, San Diego, CA.

Dr. Ma Lan has 10 peer review publications to her credit in the fields of transplant immunology and laser vascular surgery.

Dr. Ma Lan attained the rank of Lieutenant in the Chinese Air Force with primary responsibilities as a general surgeon in the Canton Air Force Hospital, PRC.

Alexandria Brighton, MF, MA, MB, NAHA

Ms. Brighton has worked with essential oils as a Master Formulator for more than 25 years, she is a Master Blender of essential oils, Medical Aromatherapist and a Professional Member of NAHA.

Ms. Brighton has apprenticed with the world's most highly regarded physicians who employ aromatherapy in their practice, essential oil farms, growers and distillers of essential oils to enhance her knowledge and expertise in selecting and blending essential oils and as a formulator of essential oil products.

Ms. Brighton has explored the Himalayas and India in search of unique essential oils.

Ms. Brighton is a highly regarded and sought after lecturer on the subjects of feng shui, aromatherapy and the clinical use of essential oils. Ms. Brighton has been featured as an instructor and keynote speaker for aromatherapy workshops for professional aromatherapist and the general public since 1988.

Dr. Judy Wright, ND, MH, MA, CNHP

Dr. Judy Wright is an ND (Naturopathic Doctor) and has operated a private practice since 1993 where she has employed essential oils as a primary therapeutic modality; she is a Master Herbalist, Medical Aromatherapist, Natural Health Professional and a CEU Provider.

Dr. Wright has gained international notoriety and has been instrumental in developing and formulating unique nutritional supplement products. Dr. Wright has been featured as an instructor and keynote speaker for aromatherapy and herbal workshops for professional aromatherapist and the general public since 2001.

Introduction

Essential oils or "essences" are highly concentrated volatile oils extracted from aromatic plants. The essential oils are typically extracted from the plant material (leaves, flowers, stems, bark, roots, etc.) by steam distillation, a technique first recorded in ancient Mesopotamia. Essential oils are very volatile and will literally evaporate when left exposed to the environment.

The chemical make-up of essential oils is very complex, with some oils containing hundreds of separate substances. These components include terpenes, alcohols, aldehydes and esters, which explains, why essential oils often times produce a wide variety of effects.

Essential oils have a "micro" sized droplet and molecular structure that allows them to be absorbed into the bloodstream by inhalation and trans-dermal applications.

Essential oils are legendary for their antimicrobial properties; they in fact were the "antibiotics" universally used throughout the ancient world up until World War II before the discovery of sulfa drugs and penicillin.

In addition to the medicinal properties attributed to essential oils, they are legendary for uplifting the emotions. The sense of smell begins in the first cranial nerve (the olfactory nerves) which carries the neurophytochemicals in the essential oils to the limbic system, the area of the brain that is responsible for emotion and memory. The dynamic affects of essential oil aromatherapy on the emotions has resulted in the practice of aromatherapy being dubbed "psycho-aromatherapy."

The relatively new science of psychoneuroimmunology has reported that pleasure producing experiences (i.e. - love, music, massage, fragrances) will in fact enhance the human immune system.

We believe that the use of essential oils and aromatherapy by individuals and various health practitioners in our modern societies has an important place in promoting physical and emotional health world wide. We know that you will find the information contained in Passport to Aromatherapy useful - by employing this information on a daily basis, one can save themselves an enormous amount of unnecessary misery, save a gob of money and add many healthful years to their lives.

Enjoy the journey with your

Passport to Aromatherapy

芬

Chapter 1

"Some twenty-five centuries before (Hippocrates), the Greek father of medicine, laid the foundation of modern medicine, there already existed a coherent and largely codified body of (Egyptian medical) practice that indisputably influenced the medical thought of the Hebrews, the Greeks and the Romans."

- from
Medicine in the Days of the Pharaohs

The History of Aromatherapy

Aromatherapy is a branch or subdivision of herbal medicine that specifically uses the purified essential oils and resins extracted from plants for medicinal purposes. Worldwide, there are more than 3,000 essential oils in use by various human cultures; most of these oils are used locally in their areas of origin. Approximately 300 of the classical essential oils are widely used and have been traded worldwide for millennia.

The health benefits of plant oils have been appreciated by ancient cultures for more than 6000 years.

The origins of aromatherapy began as religious, medicinal and social rites and celebrations of ancient cultures. The Chinese are thought to be the first to discover the significant medicinal properties of plants about 4500 BC. The Egyptians were credited with recognizing and vigorously exploring the physical and medicinal benefits of essential oils.

From pictoglyphs and wall paintings it is quite clear that essential oils were used as offerings to the ancient gods. The antiseptic and disinfectant features of essential oils and resins (i.e.- cedarwood and frankincense) made them perfect for the purpose of preserving corpses for their journey into the after world.

The discovery of remarkably preserved mummies 5000 years after their embalming is a testimony to the ancient embalmers skills and the effective antimicrobial properties of essential oils.

Egyptian priests learned by 3000 B.C. that the oils that they had been using for religious ceremonies and their embalming art had medicinal properties that could be used to heal the living. Common use of the essential oils spread to all levels of Egyptian society in the form of home remedies, cosmetics and perfume.

One of the founders of "pharaonic" medicine was the architect Imhotep, the Grand Vizier of King Djoser (2780 - 2720 B.C.). Imhotep is credited for instituting the use of essential oils, herbs and aromatic plants for medicinal substances.

Hieroglyphics on the walls of Egyptian temples illustrate the mixing of essential oils and list hundreds of essential oil recipes.

A sacred chamber in the Temple of Isis on the island of Philae illustrates a ritual referred to as "Cleansing the Flesh and Blood of Evil Deities." This process required three days of cleansing with essential oils.

An ancient papyrus discovered in the Temple of Edfu listed medicinal formulae and perfume recipes used by the alchemist and high priests for mixing aromatic oils and plant substances for rituals.

In antiquity a large number of notable philosophers were directly influenced by their visits to "the Land of the Eternal River." The thoughts and beliefs of Homer, Plato, Pythagoras, Plutarch, Thales, Herodotus and Solon were molded to a significant degree by their sojourns through Egyptian culture and science.

The great works of the legendary Greek and Roman philosophers provided a cultural and scientific bridge between Egyptian and Western civilization. This bloom of hybrid vigor was abruptly disconnected by the burning of the Library of Alexandria and the closing of the pagan temples of the Roman Empire by Theodosius in A.D. 391.

The destruction of the Roman temples at the same time that hieroglyphic writings had completely vanished extinguished the last vestiges of ancient Egyptian writings. During the following fourteen centuries, depictions of Egyptian civilization and culture almost all but disappeared. Egypt's architectural treasures survived wave after wave of occupying forces while its literary, artistic, medical and scientific discoveries were forgotten.

The dearth of documentary evidence and the faintness of the memory of the ancient accomplishments resulted in the origin of Western medicine being attributed to Hippocrates. In fact, 25 centuries before Hippocrates, the "father of modern medicine," laid the foundation of modern medicine, the Egyptians had already produced a regimented body of medical practice that had guided the scientific philosophy of the Hebrews, the Greeks and the Romans.

It was only towards the end of the 19th century following the discovery and the translation of papyri that contained a mixture of medical and magical elements that a wide interest in Egyptian medicine flourished. The initial translation gave rise to a long lasting myth that Egyptian medicine was nothing more than a medico-magical pseudoscience and "Oriental" "totally lacking in objective scientific value."

The Bible and Aromatherapy

There are over 200 references to aromatics, incense and ointments throughout the Old and New Testaments of the Bible. Aromatics, including frankincense, myrrh, galbanum, cinnamon, cassia, rosemary, hyssop and spikenard were used for anointing and healing the sick and infirm.

In Exodus, the Lord gave a recipe to Moses for a Holy anointing oil:

Myrrh "five hundred shekels" (approx. I gallon)

Cinnamon "two hundred and fifty shekels"

Calamus "two hundred and fifty shekels"

Cassia "five hundred shekels"

Olive oil "an hin" (approx 1 1/3 gallons)

Psalm 133:2 makes reference to the sweetness of the brethren dwelling together in unity: "*It is like the precious ointment upon the head, that ran down the beard, even Aaron's beard: that went down to the skirts of his garments.*"

In Ecclesiastes 9:8: "*Let thy garments be always white; and let thy head lack no ointment.*"

The Bible records an incident where an incense offering by Aaron thwarted a plague. In Numbers 16:46-50 testifies that Moses instructed Aaron to take a censer, add burning coals and incense, and to "*go quickly into the congregation to make an atonement for them: for there is a wrath gone out from the Lord; the plague is begun.*"

The Bible records that Aaron stood between the dead and the living and the plague was stopped.

The biblical and Talmudic recipes for incense contained three varieties of cinnamon. The incense ingredient listed as "stacte" is believed to be a sweet, myrrh-related spice.

Long before the time of Christ, the ancient Egyptians collected essential oils and placed them in alabaster jars. These jars were carved and shaped for storing scented oils.

In 1817, the Ebers Papyrus, a medical scroll over 870 feet long, was discovered. Dating back to 1500 B.C., the scroll listed over 800 different herbal prescriptions and remedies. Additional scrolls described a high rate of success in treating 81 separate diseases. Many mixtures contained myrrh and honey.

In 1922, when King Tut's tomb was opened, more than 50 alabaster jars crafted to hold 350 liters of oils were discovered.

Most viruses, fungi and bacteria are killed by common essential oils, especially those rich in phenols, carvacrol, thymol and terpenes. The presence of these phytochemicals in essential oils can explain why Moses used aromatic oils to protect the Israelites from the plagues that wiped out the ancient Egyptians.

The physicians of Ionia, Attia and Crete came to the cities of the Nile to increase their knowledge. At this same time, the school of Cos was founded and was attended by Hippocrates (460 - 377 B.C.).

Hippocrates recorded the Greeks use of essential oils and their sedative and stimulant properties. The Greeks and the Romans used aromatic essential oils in religious rites and ceremonies. The wide spread use of essential oils in public bathes and for massage purposes spread general knowledge about aromatherapy.

In Mark 14:3 the anointing of Jesus is described: "*And being in Bethany in the house of Simon the leper, as he sat at meat, there came a woman having an alabaster box of ointment of spikenard very precious; and she brake the box, and poured it on his head.*"

The anointing of Jesus is also described in John 12:3: "*Then took Mary a pound of ointment of spikenard, very costly, and anointed the feet of Jesus, and wiped his feet with her hair: and the house was filled with the odour of the ointment.*"

Cleopatra, the legendary queen of Egypt, is known to have soaked the sails of her royal barge in rose essence so that the perfume would drift down river on the breeze to herald her arrival to Mark Anthony who waited with anticipation on the banks of the River Nile.

The fall of the Roman Empire brought an end to the general use of essential oils in Europe. The art and science in the use of essential oils in the rest of the world continued to grow, especially in Arabia.

Avicenna, the great Arab physician was the first to distill the essential oils from roses in 1000 A.D. Arabia became the center of all knowledge for the production of high quality perfumes, importing raw materials from Egypt, India, Tibet and China and then trading the finished essential oil products world wide.

The Crusaders reintroduced the concept and art of essential oils and perfumes back into Europe during the 12th century. The records show that aromatic essential oils were used to ward off the plague and lower the rate of death amongst the producers of medicinal oils and perfumes.

The 12th century mystic, Hildegard of Bingen, used herbs and essential oils frequently in her famous healings. Hildegard, a Benedictine nun founded her own convent and was the author of a number of scholarly works including her book, *Physica*, which had more than 200 chapters that described plants and their importance in the process of healing.

The 15th century ushered in the return and widespread popularity of the medicinal essential oils and perfumes in Europe. During the devastating plagues of the 15th century a notorious band of thieves and grave robbers, who were spice traders and perfumers during the day, were protected from being infected with the plague as they robbed the bodies of the dead by covering themselves with essential oils that had antimicrobial properties.

By the 17th century the aphrodisiac properties of the essential oils were widely recognized.

Nicholas Culpeper, the legendary 17th century English herbalist, accumulated data on the medicinal value of herbs and essential oils and laid the modern foundation for their widespread use as home remedies.

Essential oils are an integral part of Americana. Pharmacist John Pemberton created Coca Cola in May 1886. He flavored the "nerve tonic" with the essential oils of orange, lemon, nutmeg, cinnamon, coriander and neroli. The flavoring part of Coca Cola is known as "7X." The seventh ingredient, a "trade secret," was thought to be the extract of vanilla or lime oil.

The term "Aromatherapie" was first coined in 1928 by Rene'-Maurice Gattefosse', a French cosmetic chemist, to describe the therapeutic action of aromatic plant essences.

Dr. Gattefosse' wrote a book, *Aromatherapy*, that was published in 1937. In his legendary book he tells his story of how he used lavender essential oils to heal a serious burn:

Dr. Gattefosse' was literally aflame - covered in burning substances - following a laboratory explosion in July 1910. After he extinguished the flames by rolling on a grassy lawn, he wrote that "both my hands were covered with rapidly developing gas gangrene." Dr. Gattefosse' said that "just one rinse with lavender essence stopped the gasification of the tissue. This treatment was followed by profuse sweating and healing which began the next day."

This early work in the area of aromatherapy as a science was advanced by Dr. Jean Valnet who discovered the essential oils had considerable levels of regenerative and antiseptic properties effective in healing the wounds of World War II soldiers.

The general application and widespread use of aromatherapy for beauty therapy and home remedies in modern times was pioneered by Marguerite Maury in her book, The Secret of Life and Youth. She also developed modern techniques for applying the essential oils through massage.

In the 21st century, there is a world wide resurgence and increase in interest in the art of aromatherapy; and up to date analytical research is beginning to uncover and support the scientific basis of the benefits and applications that had been accumulated by trial and error over thousands of years.

Chapter 2

"The Egyptians used potions, gargles and mouthwashes, herbal teas, various decoctions and steepings, pills, lozenges, pellets, poultices, ointments, ophthalmic and auricular salves, plasters, eye drops, inhalations, fumigations, suppositories, enemas, tampons and vaginal injections."

- from

Medicine in the Days of the Pharaohs

The Use of Essential Oils

The critical element in any aromatherapy treatment program is the pure essential oil. Essential oils are considerably different than the crude plant oils used in cooking, they are concentrated "essences" that are highly volatile and highly flammable.

Even though essential oils are referred to as "oils," they are not oily. Some essential oils are thick and viscous, some are solid (resins); most are in fact watery.

The color of essential oils varies considerably; most range from clear to yellow, some like carrot is orange, spikenard can be green and German chamomile is a deep blue.

Essential oils evaporate rapidly, thus requiring that, they must be mixed with other heavier oils in order to produce a slower and more controlled release.

Because essential oils are so concentrated, the therapeutic dosage is measured in drops.

Essential Oil Chemistry

The complex molecular structure of essential oils imparts a unique antimicrobial property to them. They are able to inhibit the growth of and kill bacteria, viruses, yeast and fungi.

In 1985 Dr. Jean C. Lapraz reported that no known microorganism could survive in the essential oils of cinnamon or oregano.

According to Dr. Daniel Penoel and Pierre Franchomme the essential oils of ravensara, melissa, oregano, mountain savory, clove, cumin, cistus, hyssop and frankincense have powerful antibacterial properties.

The aromatic constituents of essential oils (i.e.- terpenes, monoterpenes, phenols, aldehydes, etc.) are made up of complex chains of carbon and hydrogen atoms that form ring structures:

Terpenes: Terpenes are a broad group of essential oil chemicals that have a variety of physiological and psychological actions in the body. Common terpenes include limonene (an antiviral phytochemical found in 90 percent of citrus essential oils); pinene, an antiseptic found in significant levels in pine and turpentine oils; and chamazulene and farnesol that posses anti-inflammatory properties come from chamomile essences.

Esters: Esters are the most common phytochemicals found in plant essences - they include linalyl acetate found in clary sage and lavender and geranyl acetate found in sweet marjoram.

Aldehydes: Aldehydes are commonly found in lemon-scented essential oils including lemongrass and citronella - they tend to posses sedative and "uplifting" qualities.

Ketones: Ketones are a double-edged sword as some contain toxic properties as well as medicinally useful factors. Mugwort, tansy, wormwood and common sage contain varying levels of the high risk thujone; pennyroyal contains the potentially dangerous ketone pulegone. Non-toxic ketones include jasmine, from jasmine; and fenchone in sweet fennel.

Alcohols: A common alcohol found in essential oils is linalool (commonly found in lavender); citronellol (commonly found in rose, lemon, eucalyptus and geranium); and geraniol (commonly found in geranium and palmarosa). They tend to have effective antiseptic and antiviral activity plus an uplifting property.

Phenols: Phenols are strong antimicrobial substances. Common irritating phenols include eugenol (cloves); thymol (thyme); and carvacrol (oregano). Anethole (fennel) and estragole (tarragon) are not irritating.

Oxides: Oxides are common components found in camphor containing essential oils. They are found in rosemary, eucalyptus, tea tree and cajuput - they tend to have expectorant effects.

Essential oils are structurally and chemically different than fatty acids - by contrast to the simple long carbon chain structure of fatty acids, essential oils have complex aromatic ring structures and contain sulfur and nitrogen atoms missing from simple fatty acids.

The terpenoids found in many essential oils are composed from the same basic structure as the five carbon isoprene molecule. Two isoprene units linked together form monoterpenes; when three isoprene units are connected they form sesquiterpenes, etc.

Some of the largest molecules found in essential oils are triterpenoids consisting of 30 carbon atoms or six isoprene units joined together.

Carotenoids consisting of 40 carbon atoms or eight isoprene units are only found in small quantities in essential oils because the molecule is too large to be extracted by simple steam distillation.

Essential oils are comprised of many different active molecules, each of which can produce their own physiological effect. German chamomile (*Matricaria recutita*) contains azulene, a dark blue substance that produces powerful anti-inflammatory effects. German chamomile additionally contains bisobolol, a compound with potent sedative affects.

Methods of Application

There are three basic models for the delivery of essential oil aromatherapy.

The English model promotes the dilution of a small amount of the essential oil in a base or carrier oil and massaging the mix into the skin for the purpose of relaxation and stress relief.

The French approach advocates the ingestion of and the undiluted topical application of therapeutic grade essential oils. The French will typically add a few drops of an essential oil to honey, a small piece of bread or a small amount of carrier oil.

The German model focuses on the inhalation of the vapors of essential oils.

The three classic methods of delivery of essential oils can be combined into the inhalation, auricular technique, touch therapy, spinal touch, lymphatic massage to maximize the benefit and outcome of the therapy.

Safety Guidelines

There are critical safety guidelines to adhere to when using essential oils, especially if you are unfamiliar with the oils, their benefits and hazards. The beginner should use common sense and start gradually to accumulate experience.

1. Always keep a one quart bottle of corn oil handy for an emergency when using pure essential oils. Vegetable oils easily dilute essential oils to prevent serious skin irritation. You can't efficiently dilute essential oils on the skin with water.

2. Keep bottles of essential oils tightly closed and store them in a cool location away from light. If stored properly, essential oils will maintain their effectiveness and potency for many years.

3. Keep essential oils out of the reach of children. Treat essential oils securely like you would any other medicine in the medicine cabinet.

4. Essential oils and essential oil blends rich in menthol (i.e. -peppermint) should not be used on the throat or neck of children under three years of age.

5. Angelica, bergamot, grapefruit, lemon, orange, tangerine and other citrus oils can produce a photosensitive reaction and may cause a rash or dark pigmentation on skin exposed to direct sunlight or UV rays within three to four days after application.

6. Keep essential oils away from the eye and never put them directly into the ears. Do not handle contact lenses or rub eyes with essential oils on your fingers. Oils with a high phenol content (i.e. -oregano, cinnamon, thyme, clove, lemongrass and bergamot) may damage contact lenses and will irritate eyes.

7. Pregnant women should consult a health care professional when considering any type of health program that would include essential oils.

8. Individuals with seizure disorders and those with hypertension should consult their health care professional before using essential oils. Use special caution when using hyssop, fennel, basil, wintergreen/birch, nutmeg, rosemary, peppermint, sage or tarragon essential oils.

9. People with allergies should test a small amount of oil on an area of sensitive skin, such as the inside of the upper arm, before applying the oil more widely on the body. The bottom of the feet is one of the safest, most effective places to apply essential oils.

10. Before taking GRAS (Generally Regarded As Safe) essential oils internally, dilute one drop of essential oil in one teaspoon of an oil soluble liquid such as honey, olive oil or soy oil. Never consume more than a few drops of an essential oil on any single day without the advice of a health professional.

11. Do not add undiluted essential oils directly to bath water. Use a proper base oil/essential oil blend in your bath water; this is a safe way to disperse essential oils in your bath.

12. Keep essential oils away from open flames, sparks, electric appliances and electric outlets. Some essential oils such as orange, white fir, pine and peppermint are particularly flammable.

Terms

Essence: Essential oils are considered to be the "living" substances and elements of a plant. The process of extraction of essential oils from the plant is a delicate process. Certain petals, leaves and other plant parts must be harvested at exactly the precise moment, or the quality and usefulness of the oil is severely affected. Only the purest of essences can be effectively used for aromatherapy to be able to maximize and predict the outcome and effectiveness.

Essential oils are extracted from a wide variety of plant parts, including petals, leaves, seeds, nuts, bark, stalks, flower heads, gums and resins.

Essential oils are used by inhaling their vapors, applying them topically via massage and adding them to a therapeutic bath.

Essential oils have a small molecular structure allowing them to easily penetrate the skin, oral and intestinal mucosal lining.

Having been used for medicinal purposes for thousands of years, essential oils are well established as an effective home remedy for the relief of many health problems.

How do Essential Oils Work

Essential oils are comprised of a collection of small molecules that are easily dissolved in a variety of solvents including alcohol, emulsifiers and lipids.

Essential oils are not simple substances, they are "mosaics" of hundreds or sometimes thousands of individual phytochemicals. Indi-

Comparative Antibacterial Properties of Essential Oils and Antibiotics

Substance	Loading Levels (ul)*	Escherichia coli	Staphylococcus aureus
		Zone of Inhibition (cm)	
Penicillin	3	0	3.2
	6	0	3.4
	8	0	3.6
	12	0	3.6
Ampicillin	3	1.9	2.6
	6	2.1	2.6
	8	2.5	2.7
	12	2.6	2.8
Cinnamon	3	2.4	2.4
	6	2.8	2.8
	8	-	3.0
	12	3.0	3.2
Oregano	3	2.6	3.2
	6	3.3	3.6
	8	-	3.6
	12	3.3	3.8

* The concentration of penicillin = 1.76 units/ul
The concentration of ampicillin = 5 ug/ ul

vidual oils may contain a range of 80 - 300 phytochemicals.

These highly volatile essential oils begin to evaporate as soon as the container is opened allowing them to be inhaled and absorbed through the mucosa of the nasal passages and immediately begin to send chemical messages to the brain. The essential oils affect the limbic system of the brain which controls an individual's emotions and major functions of the body.

Aromatherapy is known to enhance the individual's physical, biochemical, mental and psychological status concurrently. Each individual essential oil has a specific biochemical "fingerprint" that determines its characteristic fragrance, color, volatility, biological and physiological properties.

Harvest Methods

Distillation: The Egyptians placed the fresh plant material into large clay or alabaster pots; water was added to the pots; the pots were heated to produce steam that was directed through a cotton cloth plugging the neck of the jar.

The cotton plug collected the essential oil; the cotton plug was then pressed and the oil was collected into another vessel.

In the 21st century, high-pressure steam is passed over and through the leaves, bark, roots and flowers in modern stills that have an attached vacuum process that encourages maximum production of the oils.

The steam carrying the essential oil vapors is passed through a cooling chamber; the oil condenses out and is easily separated from the water condensate.

Maceration: Flowers are soaked in heated oil to break down the plant cellular structure to release the essential oils into the collecting oil, which is then distilled to separate the essential oil from the collecting oil.

Enfleurage: Delicate plants and plant materials such as jasmine, neroli and rose produce minimal amounts of their essential oils. These delicate and low volume oils are collected by crushing the raw plant material between wooden-framed, glass trays smeared with animal fats until the fat is saturated with the essential oils. This final product can be used as is or the essential oils separated out by distillation.

Pressing: Pressing is a simple mechanical method of squeezing the essential oils from plant material by means of a press; this method is usually limited to extracting the essential oils from the rinds and peels of ripe fruit including lemon and orange into a sponge.

Quality Control

As the plants, flowers and plant parts are harvested they should be processed and stored quickly to prevent oxidation and loss of the essential oils through evaporation.

Climate, soil quality and altitude can have a dynamic effect on the quality and character of an essential oil. For example, the aroma and quality of French lavender oil can vary considerably year by year in a manner similar to the aroma and quality of a particular wine year.

Essential oils can be distilled or extracted by many different ways that can have dramatic effects on their chemistry and medicinal properties.

Oils that are distilled several times are not as potent as oils that are only distilled once.

Oils that are subjected to high heat and pressure wind up with a very simple and limited profile of phytochemicals. Excessive heat and temperature fractures and breaks down many of the fragile aromatic compounds that are characteristic of essential oils.

Essential oils that are steam distilled are considerably different in character than the same oils that are extracted by solvent extraction.

There are serious concerns that many commercially available essential oils are adulterated, engineered or extended with synthetic chemicals. A typical example is frankincense that has been "extended" with colorless and odorless solvents including diethylphthalate or dipropylene glycol.

The best way to assure the purchase of the purest and highest quality essential oils is to ask to see the analysis of the essential oil product that has been subjected to gas chromatography, mass spectroscopy and NMRI testing.

E.O.B.B.D.

Essental oils of unknown origin or of questionable quality are commonly sold in the "recreational" aromatherapy market. By contrast, a therapeutic grade essential oil can be traced back to a particular field, year, and distiller - additionally the specific chemical analysis must be available.

The E.O.B.B.D. (Essential Oils Botanically and Biochemically Defined) label is a guarantee of quality and purity. This label is only given by the I.N.S.A. (Institute de Normalization Scientifique D'Aromatologie), a committee of independent European health professionals.

Criteria for Rejecting Essential Oils for Therapeutic Use

1) Deterpened essential oil

2) Chemically reconstructed essential oil

3) Adulterated essential oil (synthetic aromatics added)

4) Essential oil diluted with oil of lesser value

5) Essential oil extracted with organic solvents

6) Burned essential oil (distilled at temperatures that are too high)

The highest quality oils tend to be more expensive, however, as with all things you get what you pay for.

Aromatherapy Terms

Inhalation: Steam and vapor inhalation is a classic method for relieving respiratory problems including colds, bronchitis and the flu. Add six to twelve drops of the essential oil to a bowl of steaming hot water. Place a towel over your head in a tent-like fashion over the bowl and breathe deeply. In addition this is a good way to deep clean the facial skin.

Therapeutic Massage: This is the most common and most efficient method of delivering the benefits of aromatherapy. Message with essential oils support the body's healing processes through lymphatic massage and the stimulation of blood and lymphatic circulation. The aromas released during the massage also affect the limbic system, the emotional center of the brain. Use a one to three percent solution of essential oil to the base massage oil.

Acupuncture: Acupuncturists can significantly increase the positive result of their treatment by adding essential oils to their technique. Dip the tip of the acupuncture needle into the appropriate essential oil before inserting it.

Acupressure: Apply one to three drops of an essential oil to the acupressure point with a fingertip. Start by pressing firmly and releasing. Avoid applying pressure to any particular pressure point too long. After completing small point stimulation, massage the general area with the oil.

Fragrancers: These simple pots, also called diffusers or vaporizers are easy to use. Fill the top china or clay bowl with water and add two or three drops of essential oil to the surface of the water. The candle under the water vessel heats the water, slowly releasing the essential oil vapors into the room. For safety place the candle on a plate or tile. It is also possible to purchase battery driven or car cigarette lighter driven fan vaporizers that blow air through oil impregnated pads.

Baths: Fill tub half full with "hand hot" water (104 degrees F), add five to ten drops of the chosen essential oil. Close the bathroom door to fill the small room with steam and the oils essence. Soak in the tub for 15 minutes or until the water cools to just below body temperature.

People with sensitive skin should dilute the essential oil in a base oil (i.e. - almond, apricot or peach pit).

Foot Bath: Tired feet can get relief and be refreshed by adding four to five drops of peppermint, rosemary and thyme to a large bowl of hot water; lavender can be used to soothe tired feet.

Hand Bath: Chapped skin can be soothed and healed by soaking in a bowl of "warm" water; add three to four drops of patchouli or comfrey.

Shower: Soap well during a warm shower; rinse well. Dip a wet sponge in an oil mix; squeeze and rub oil mix over entire body while still under warm shower.

Sauna: Add two drops of eucalyptus or pine oil per one half pint of water and throw on the heat source to produce steam and essential oil vapors to cleanse and detoxify the body.

Jacuzzi and hot tub: Add 10 - 15 drops of sandalwood, geranium or ylang-ylang oils to the hot tub to relax; stimulate the body with the oils of pine, rosemary and neroli added to the hot tub.

Room Sprays: Add 10 to 12 drops of individual or essential oil mixes or blends to four ounces of distilled water. Shake well and then fill sprayer.

"Pillow Talk": Perfume pillow with two to three drops of oil; add two to three drops of essential oil to a facial tissue and place it into the pillow case to avoid getting the oil into the eyes; choose a relaxing oil to relieve insomnia and to promote sleep; add an aphrodisiac such as ylang-ylang, rose or jasmine to promote a romantic evening.

Perfumes: The finest and most expensive perfumes are typically blended from the purist of essential of essential oils from flower extracts.

Pomanders: Hang corked clay bottles in your closet or wardrobe. Fill the jar with a favorite essential oil; use Melissa, bergamot or cedarwood to repel moths. The essential oil is absorbed by the clay and then released slowly into the closet space.

Pot Pourri: Add three to five drops of an aromatic, flowery or spicy essential oil to revitalize exhausted pot pourri or better yet make your own.

Handkerchief: The old dependable and humble handkerchief is the most "portable" method of applying essential oils. Add three to four drops on the handkerchief, cover nose and inhale. This simple method of delivery is useful for relieving colds, bronchitis, sinusitis and headaches.

Shoe Rack: Freshen your closet with the essential oil of lemongrass. Deodorize shoes with two to five drops of pine or parsley oils.

Humidifiers: Add five to ten drops of eucalyptus or tea tree oil to the humidifier water or to a small bowl of water and place on heat vents or radiator.

Ring Burners: Ring burners employ the heat from standard incandescent bulbs to vaporize essential oils. Small ring burners made from porcelain sit on the rounded top of the bulb; add two to five drops of the chosen essential oil and the heat from the bulb will disperse the vapors into the room (a potential disadvantage of the ring burners is that bulbs larger than 40 watts can quickly evaporate, burn or oxidize the oils).

Wood Fires: Sprinkle several drops of cypress, cedarwood, pine or sandalwood oils on the logs to be burned an hour before kindling the fire. The burning logs will vaporize the oils and fill the room with the essential oils.

Scented Candles: High quality wax candles can be purchased already laced with essential oils - "aroma therapy candles." Essential oils can be added to the oil reservoir of an oil lamp for a similar effect.

Warm Compresses: Soak a clean cotton wash clothe with warm water and add five to ten drops of the chosen essential oil. Wring out excess fluid and cover the area to be treated. Cover with a dry terry clothe towel until cool; they can be used to relieve headaches, sinus headaches, sprains, bruises and hot flashes.

Cold Packs: Apply cold water or ice packs to inflamed or swollen tissue (i.e. - sprain, strain, bruise, etc.) previously treated with essential oils. Packages of frozen vegetables can be used as cold packs. Maintain the cold pack in position until the swelling and redness is reduced.

Body and Facial oils: Use a one percent blend of essential oil to carrier oils on the face and a three percent blend on the body to nourish and soothe the skin.

Layering: Instead of a blend apply several oils one after the other - for instance apply marjoram to sore muscles, massage area until area is dry; then apply second oil such as peppermint, massage until the area is dry; thirdly apply basil and massage until area is dry.

Vaginal Retention Implant: To effectively relieve candida or vaginitis, employ a vaginal implant to deliver essential oils:

1. Place 10-20 drops of essential oil into a tablespoon of carrier oil.

2. While lying down, use a small syringe to deliver the oil mix into the vagina when retiring. Do not get up until morning.

3. A capsule may be used as a suppository - place oils in the capsule and implant quickly after the oils are added.

4. A pad or tampon can help retain the oil blend in the vagina.

Rectal Implant: Rectal implants and retention enemas are the best methods of getting essential oils to the urinary tract and reproductive organs. Use sterile applicator:

1. Mix 20-35 drops of essential oil in a teaspoon of carrier oil.

2. Place oil mix in a small syringe, lubricate delivery end of syringe, insert into rectum and deliver into the rectum.

3. Retain mixture through the night.

4. Clean and disinfect syringe or applicator tip after each use.

Glossary of Herbal and Essential Oil Terms

Analgesic: reduces or eliminates pain.

Antibiotic/Antibacterial: inhibits bacterial growth.

Antifungal: inhibits fungal growth.

Anti-infectious: inhibits infection.

Antiparasitic: inhibits or repels insect/arachnid parasites.

Antiputrescent: inhibits putrefaction.

Antisclerotic: inhibits hardening of cells and tissue.

Antiseborrheic: reduces and inhibits excessive secretions of the sebaceous glands.

Antiseptic: destroys microbes and inhibits their proliferation.

Antispasmodic: prevents and reduces spasms, convulsions and severe contractions.

Antisudorific: inhibits sweating.

Antitoxic: reduces and counteracts the effects of toxins, particularly bacterial.

Antitussive: inhibits and relieves coughs.

Antivenomous: reduces or counteracts the effects of venom.

Antiviral: inhibits viral growth.

Balsamic: soothes sore throats and relieves coughs originating in the throat.

Calmative: sedative, calming agent.

Carminative: relieves flatulence; reduces abdominal discomfort and bloating.

Cholagogue: promotes the release of bile from the gall bladder and bile ducts.

Cicatrisive: promotes healing and the formation of scar tissue.

Cytophylactic: promotes cell proliferation and healing.

Depurative: cleanser, detoxifier; "purifies" and "cleanses" the blood and internal organs.

Diuretic: promotes the elimination of excess water from the body via the urinary system.

Emmenagogue: initiates, induces or regulates menstruation.

Emollient: soothes and softens the skin.

Expectorant: promotes removal of mucus from the respiratory system.

Febrifuge: reduces or inhibits fever.

Galactagogue: induces and encourages the flow of breast milk.

Haemostatic: stops bleeding.

Hepatic: supports the healthy function of the liver.

Immunostimulant: supports and modulates the immune system.

Mucolytic: breaks down mucus.

Nervine: supports healthy nerve function; can relieve symptoms of nervous disorders.

Pectoral: relieves symptoms of diseases or conditions of the chest and respiratory system.

Rubefacient: a counter-irritant used to increase circulation in a particular area; results in redness of the area of skin it is applied to.

Sedative: reduces mental excitement and encourages calmness.

Soporific: induces restfulness and encourages sleep.

Stimulant: increases metabolic and mental processes of the brain and body.

Stomachic: enhances function of the stomach; it is a gastric tonic and digestive aid.

Tonic: invigorates, refreshes and supports mental and body functions.

Vagotonic: supports healthy activity of tissues innervated by the 10th cranial (vagus) nerve.

Vasodilator: increases blood flow throughout the body by dilating the vascular system.

Vermifuge: expels intestinal parasites (worms).

Vulnerary: heals wounds, ulcers and sores by external, topical application.

Chapter 3

"Medicinal preparations were often long, complicated, and above all very numerous, as though Egyptian practitioners hoped by multiplying them to achieve the greatest possible (broad spectrum) effectiveness, fortified still further by the recitation of magical formulas."

- from

Medicine in the Days of the Pharaohs

Blending, Mixing and Pesticides

Essential oils are the basic "tools" used in traditional aroma therapy. Each one is unique and has a specific fragrance and "fingerprint" affect on the mind and body.

Aromatherapy Families

Citrus: Bergamot, grapefruit, lemon, lime, mandarin, orange.

Floral: Geranium, chamomile, rose otto, lavender, ylang-ylang, neroli.

Herbaceous: Chamomile, lavender, rosemary, peppermint, marjoram, clary sage.

Champhoraceous: Eucalyptus, cajeput, rosemary, peppermint and tea tree.

Spicy: Coriander, black pepper, ginger and cardamom.

Resinous: Frankincense, elemi, myrrh and galbanum.

Woody: Cedarwood, sandalwood, pine, juniper berries, Cypress.

Earthy: Patchouli and vetiver.

The art of combining two or more essential oils enlists the arts of the perfumier and the pharmacist.

Avoid trying to smell essential oils directly from the original storage container. To check the aroma of an essential oil, place one drop in a tablespoon or on the side of a glass.

Base or Carrier Oils

Base or carrier oils are a basic part of aroma therapy. The essential oils should be measured in drops and placed in a base or carrier oil before use.

Carrier oils are rich in nutrients, including vitamin E and omega-3 essential fatty acids.

The base oil dilutes the essential oil, slows the rate of evaporation, reduces skin irritation and allows for an even spread over the area to be treated.

Use a glass or porcelain jar or bottle filled with the carrier oil before you add the drops of essential oils to the mix - use an eye dropper to ensure accurate doses.

Base or carrier oils are commonly extracted from nuts or seeds and each has its own peculiar benefit.

Sweet almond oil is considered the best all-purpose carrier oil as it is neutral and has minimal allergenic properties. It is safe enough to use to massage babies.

Walnut oil has the properties of a "coordinator." Walnut oil balances the nervous system and can help relieve dysmenorrhea.

Sesame oil is particularly useful for reducing stretch marks.

Apricot kernel oil, peach kernel oil and evening primrose oils are useful as general tonics and can stimulate cell regeneration.

Wheat germ oil provides anti-oxidant properties and will help preserve an essential oil blend.

Summary of Carrier or Base Oils

Almond Oil (*Prunus amygdalis var. dulcis*): The highest quality almond oil is "warm pressed" from the kernels of the sweet almond tree. One can also extract a "fixed" oil and an essential oil from bitter almonds, *Prunus dulcis var. amara.* During the extraction procedures, cyanide or prussic acid is oftentimes created. Commercial bitter almond extract is "rectified" to remove the prussic acid.

Apricot Kernel Oil (*Prunus armenica*): Apricot kernel oil is a light oil that is used primarily in beauty and skin care products.

Avocado Oil (*Persea americana*): Avocado oil is a rich penetrating oil that is used primarily in beauty and skin care products.

Castor Oil (*Ricinus communis*): Castor oil is a thick, sticky oil that is often used in hair products.

Coconut Oil (*Cocus nucifera*): Coconut oil is a light, odorless, highly refined oil obtained by solvent extraction of dried coconut meat. Most coconut oil is classically a soft buttery semi-solid at room temperature, however, a fractionated coconut oil that keeps its liquid form in even cool temperatures.

Corn Oil (*Zea mays*): Corn oil is warm-pressed from sweet corn kernels. It is vivid yellow in color, sticky and emits a very a low but distinct cooked corn scent.

Evening Primrose Oil (*Oenothera biennis*): Evening primrose oil is a "fine textured" oil that emits a "musty" aroma.

Grape seed Oil (*Vitis vinifera*): Grape seed oil has a light green color and is odorless, therefore it is a common carrier oil for aromatherapy.

Peanut (Groundnut) Oil (*Arachis hypogaea*): Peanut oil has a nutty odor and sticky texture.

Hazelnut (Filbert) Oil (*Corylus avellana*): Hazelnut oil is warm pressed from hazelnuts or filberts, and is classically a strong, sweet, nutty smelling oil. It is commonly used in beauty care products.

Jojoba Oil (*Simmondsia chinensis*): Jojoba oil is in fact a liquid wax that is commonly used in beauty care products.

Macadamia Oil (*Macadamia integrifolia and M. ternifolia*): Macadamia oil is a rich nourishing oil that is commonly used in beauty care products.

Olive Oil (*Olea europaea*): The dark yellow-green oil is classically extracted from hard unripe olives and has a fruity-peppery aroma - it is typically diluted by half with oils less odorous.

Passionflower Oil (*Passiflora incarnate*): Passionflower oil is extracted from the seeds and is typically used in beauty products.

Safflower Oil (*Carthamus tinctorius*): Safflower oil is extracted by the warm-press technique from the seeds; it has a golden-yellow color and a slight nutty odor.

Sesame Oil (*Sesamum indicum*): Sesame oil is warm pressed from sesame seeds; it is golden yellow, slightly bitter with a nutty smell.

Soy Oil (*Glycine soja*): Soy oil is extracted from the beans by a solvent process as they contain only small amounts of oil.

Sunflower Oil (*Helianthus annus*): Sunflower oil is commonly warm pressed from the seeds; it is golden yellow with a mild sweet and nutty smell.

Wheatgerm Oil (*Triticum vulgare*): Wheatgerm oil is warm pressed or solvent extracted from the "germ" of the wheat; the oil is thick and sticky, it has an orange-brown color and an "earthy" smell.

Insecticides and Pesticides

The avoidance and reduction of chemicals in one's food and environment is essential to a longer and healthier life. It is therefore of great importance to have safe options and alternatives to dangerous household chemicals, insecticides and pesticides.

Aroma therapy repellents, insecticides and pesticides can be delivered and applied by a variety of means including spray bottles.

General Household Spray: The purpose of a general all-purpose spray is to lighten the overall load of pests before they enter your home:

1/2 tsp eucalyptus oil
1/2 tsp peppermint oil
1/4 tsp lemon oil
4 oz white vinegar

Place all oils and vinegar in a small blender and blend for 30 seconds; pour into airtight glass spray bottle; shake vigorously before each use.

Insecticide, Bug and Pest Repellent: In general, one can kill and repel insects, bugs and pests (i.e. - dust mites, lice, fleas, ticks, ants, spiders, mice, etc.) by using essential oils and oil blends including lavender, lemon, peppermint, lemongrass, cypress, eucalyptus, cinnamon, thyme, basil and citronella.

To protect stored linens from moths use citronella, lavender, lemongrass, Canadian red cedar or rosemary.

A sachet can be constructed by putting several drops of the essential oils on a cotton ball; wrap and tie up in a small handkerchief or square of cotton. Hang the sachet in a closet, chest of linens or storage area - refresh as often as necessary.

Repellents: Aromatherapy fragrances work as "repellents" by masking the odors that normally attract insects to food. A strong aroma creates a "scent shield" that covers the odors that insects are seeking - as the insect approaches your garden, your house or you they are met by the overpowering aroma of an essential oil so they move on to more attractive pickings.

One can also employ aromas that are actually repulsive to insects as a repellent.

Ants are very straight forward to deal with because they move in military formations or on multilane "highways" much like a German autobahn. Spray the essential oil mix along the ant's trail to confuse them; you can make ant-free zones by cutting new dish sponges into one half inch squares, place five drops of your essential oil mix onto each of the sponge squares and place them into the corners of your cabinets and food storage closets. A typical ant repellent made from essential oils should look like this:

Camphor
Orange
Pine
Peppermint
Spruce
Cedarwood

Flies and mosquitoes can be a challenge to deal with because they can fly around, over or under your best defenses. In the old days, people would dangle bundles of pungent herbs such as anise, bay and garlic over the windows and doors to discourage flies and mosquitoes. A typical flying insect repellent made from essential oils should look like this:

Anise
Bay
Cedarwood
Cloves
Eucalyptus
Orange

Fly and mosquito repellent that can be applied **topically** to your skin requires a different approach:

1/4 tsp citronella oil
1/4 tsp eucalyptus oil
1/8 tsp cedarwood oil
1/8 tsp geranium oil
2 oz vodka

Blend ingredients and store in a glass container; apply to exposed skin, especially the head and ankles.

The itch and pain of insect bites can be relieved by applying a topical mix of:

1/2 tsp lavender oil
1/2 tsp tea tree oil
1 Tblsp vodka

Blend ingredients; store in a glass bottle; apply directly to bites as needed.

Fleas and ticks can infest humans as well as pets; fleas can act as a carrier of tape worms. A great flea and tick repellent can be made from individual and blends of certain essential oils:

Bay laurel
Camphor
Chamomile
Citronella
Clove
Eucalyptus
Lavender
Lemon

A flea collar can be made by applying the essential oils directly to a flat braided string or rope depending on the size of the dog; the repellent affect can last as long as a week:

4 drops eucalyptus oil

Apply the essential oils along the entire string or rope and let it dry for one half hour; tie the essential oil impregnated "flea collar" around the dog's neck.

Cockroaches like damp dark hideouts, so you will want to concentrate your repellents near and in drains and in kitchen, basement and garage storage places. A typical roach repellent made from essential oils should look like this:

Angelica
Eucalyptus
Peppermint
Sage

Moths are legendary for chewing holes in woolen clothes hung in a closet or stored in a chest. The typical "mothball" contains naphthalene and or paradichlorobenzene - two very dangerous chemicals. According to the American Association of Poison Control Centers there are 5,000 reported mothball poisonings each year in America. A sachet that will repel moths can be made from a blend of essential oils:

Bay Laurel
Camphor
Cedarwood
Lavender
Patchouli
Sage

A general use **garden spray** made from essential oils and herbs can be applied directly to flowers, vegetables and herbs:

5 cloves garlic
1 cup water
1/2 tsp cayenne pepper
1/4 tsp peppermint oil
1/4 tsp rosemary oil
1/2 tsp liquid dishwashing detergent (environment and septic tank safe)

Mix the garlic, cayenne and the water in a blender for one minute; strain through a strainer or a paper coffee filter to ensure proper dispersal through a garden sprayer; blend in the essential oils and detergent; apply at dawn and dusk.

Lice are common external insect parasites found on younger school children and debilitated adults. Run a "nit" comb through the hair before and after washing and rinses to remove "nits" or eggs which will appear as tiny white rice-like objects attached to the hair. As a preventative wash hair vigorously with an antibacterial shampoo or hand soap and rinse with vinegar that contains one or a blend of several essential oils (Caution: be sure to test for sensitivity before applying large volumes of essential oil rinse) that can include:

Cinnamon leaf oil (high eugenol) (can be highly caustic)

Eucalyptus
Geranium
Lavender
Peppermint
Rosemary
Tea Tree
Thyme (high linalol)

Place four drops of one or more essential oils into a mix of one ounce of vinegar and one ounce of water for a preventative rinse or an environmental and furniture spray to repel lice.

To kill lice that have already infested an individual requires a more aggressive approach:

20 drops Tea Tree oil
10 drops Rosemary
10 drops Thyme (high linalol)
5 drops lavender
2 ounces of a carrier oil (olive, walnut, almond, etc.)

Combine ingredients; apply the oil/essential oil mix to well combed hair (use a "nit" comb); cover with a shower cap; wrap head with a towel; after one hour shampoo hair without adding water to remove most of the oil mix; rinse and shampoo a second time; repeat twice at one and two weeks.

Mice can be very destructive and unsanitary and they certainly indicate a breakdown in your home's perimeter defenses. A typical mouse repellent made from essential oils should look like this:

Peppermint
Spearmint
Wormwood

Classic Essential Oil Blends

1st Defense is a blend that is used to kill micro-organisms (i.e. - bacteria, viruses, fungi and yeast); it stimulates and supports the immune system: Ravensara, Niaouli, Tea Tree, Thyme Linalol, Peppermint, *Eucalyptus radiata*, Palmarosa, Oregano, Cinnamon bark, Clove.

To Be Well is a blend that specifically supports the immune system and kills viruses and bacteria. Diffuse, mist or wear; it is particularly useful for children: Thyme Linalol, Ravensara, *Eucalyptus radiata*, Lemon, Tea Tree.

Breath of Life is a blend that is particularly useful for treating colds, flu, respiratory illness, sinus problems, congestion, asthma, pulmonary problems: *Eucalyptus globulus*, *Eucalyptus radiata*, Peppermint, Ravensara, Naouli, Balsam fir, Pine, Rosemary, Marjoram, Lavender, Cypress.

Awareness is a blend that supports brain functions, mental acuity, memory and alertness: Basil, Lemon, Rosemary, Peppermint, Germanium, Rose.

Frankincense & Lavender Blend is used to promote healing and reduce scare tissue formation (use following radiation therapy and to treat burns): Frankincense and Lavender.

GI Purify is a blend used to purify and detoxify the digestive system: Ginger, Peppermint, Rosemary, Tea Tree, Cinnamon, Cypress, Thyme linalol.

Trauma is a blend that can reduce pain, swelling and inflammation: Marjoram, Helichrysum, Rosemary, Birch, Clove, Calophilium.

Oregano and Lavender this blend allows the use of oregano without the concern of irritation or burning of tissues: Wild Turkish Oregano and Lavender vera.

Deep Cleanser is a heavy duty cleanser for negative energy, rooms, bedding, etc. Use as a mist or diffuse: Sage, Pine, Lemongrass, Juniper, Cypress, Frankincense, Lemon, *Eucalyptus globulus*, *E. citriodora*, Spruce, Tea Tree, Thyme.

Dragon's Breath is a blend that is employed to neutralize negative energies found in places where violence has occurred: Sage, Juniper, Pine, Dragon's Blood oil, Spikenard, Frankincense, Cypress, Patchouli, Thyme, Cedarwood.

Robe of Light is a blend that maintains and stimulates optimal energy levels. Mist: Rose, Sandalwood, Ylang Ylang, Grapefruit, Geranium.

Sacred Place can be diffused or misted to increase positive energy: Juniper, Grapefruit, Cedarwood, Myrrh, Neroli, Rose, Clove, Rosewood, Palmarosa, Fennel, Jasmine, Birch.

Sealing Oil is an "anointing" oil used to seal doors, windows, and entrances: Spikenard, Frankincense, Sandalwood, Cedarwood, Elemi, Cypress.

Prosperity is a blend that is thought to bring increased opportunity (these blends were historically thought to be more valuable than gold); diffuse, mist or wear to energize yourself: Patchouli, Orange, Cinnamon, Ginger, Spruce, Nutmeg.

To Be Happy is a blend that promotes a "happy state of mind" Diffuse, mist or wear - particularly useful for children: Orange, Tangerine, Grapefruit, Mandarin, Rose, Spearmint.

To Be Loved is a blend that is thought to help one let go of past angers and promote love and joy; diffuse, mist or wear: Rosewood, Ylang Ylang, Sandalwood, Moroi, Patchouli, Geranium.

To Be At Peace is a blend that is thought to support the nervous system, promotes helpful sleep and reduce or eliminate addictions; helps children to be more peaceful. Diffuse, mist or wear: Tangerine, Orange, Blue Chamomile, Grapefruit, Ylang Ylang, Rosewood, Rose.

靜

Chapter 4

"Physicians treated patients with medicine and magic, separately or in combination, in order to make treatment as effective as possible by acting upon the mind of the sick person and, not incidentally, by acting in such a way that the privileges associated with the exercise of a particularly profitable profession would be reserved for an elite."

- from

Medicine in the Days of the Pharaohs

AROMATHERAPEUTIC AGENTS

The Egyptian pharmacopoeia was very wide and complete and is thought to be the progenitor of modern pharmaceutics. Medical preparations were "broad spectrum" in nature, containing numerous ingredients to ensure "the greatest possible effectiveness." Many of these ingredients remain unknown to us despite 240 translations offered by Ebbell for some 400 names of Egyptian "drugs" referred to in the Ebers Papyrus. There are also 358 agreed upon translations, 167 unconfirmed translations, 19 illegible hieroglyphics contained in Herman Grapow's study of more than 500 pharmacological substances including essential oils.

Essential oils are aromatic volatile lipids distilled from shrubs, flowers, trees, roots bushes and seeds. Simple vegetable oils are easily oxidized and rapidly become rancid and transformed into trans-fatty acids.

Essential oils can't become rancid, they are not "greasy" and are potent antimicrobials.

Angelica (*Angelica archangelica*)

Beginnings: Angelica originated in Syria and transplanted to France and Belgium. Known as the "holy spirit root" or the "oil of angels" by Europeans; angelica's healing powers were believed to be so strong that it was believed to be of divine origin. During the time of Paracelsus, the essential oil of angelica was known to protect against the plague. During the European plague of 1660 angelica stems were chewed to repel infection.

Description: Two similar oils are either distilled or solvent - extracted into solutes; one is derived from the seeds and the other from the roots. Key constituents:

Lemonene (60-70%)
Alpha Pinene (5-8%)
Alpha and Beta Phellandrene (3-6%)

Therapeutic Properties: Angelica has been used for a female tonic, bruises, colic, coughs, respiratory infections, indigestion, menopause, dysmenorrhea, PMS, anorexia and rheumatic discomfort.

Routes of application: The essential oils of angelica can be applied by inhalation and massage. Mixes well with patchouli, vetiver, clary sage and most citrus oils.

Caution: Consult physician before use if pregnant; avoid use if diabetic; because angelica contains bergopten, it can be photo-sensitizing and should not be applied to skin that will be exposed to direct sunlight or UV light within three to five days.

Anise (*Pimpinella anisum*)

Beginnings: Anise originated in Turkey.

Description: The essential oils are extracted by steam distillation from the seeds.

Key constituents:
Trans-Anethol (85-95%)
Methyl Chavicol (2-4%)

Therapeutic Properties: Anise is an antiseptic, antispasmodic, diuretic and stimulant.

Basil (*Ocimum basilicum*)

Beginnings: Basil was commonly used in baths and as a massage oil by Greek nobles - they particularly liked its fragrant aroma. The name basil is derived from the Greek word for king - basileus; in Ayurvedic medicine it is called tulsi. It is considered a holy herb in India, sacred to the gods Krishna and Vishnu. The Egyptians used basil as an offering to their gods and combined with essences of myrrh and frankincense it was used to embalm bodies for their passage into the "after life." The 16th century herbalist John Gerard said, "Basil's scent taketh away sorrowfulness."

Description: Basil is a native plant of Africa, Egypt, Madagascar and the Seychelles and in modern times it is commonly grown as a culinary herb in Europe. It typically is a compact bush that grows up to three feet in height and is characterized by small white to pink flowers. The oil is distilled from the leaves; it is a pale greenish-yellow in color with "sweet green overtones." Key constituents:
Methylchavicol (estragol) (40-80%)
Linalol (10-50%)
1,8 Cineole (1-7%)
Eugenol (1-10%)

Therapeutic properties: Basil is used as a nerve tonic; can be used to lift fatigue, anxiety and depression. Basil is commonly used for relieving the symptoms of bronchitis, colds, fever, gout, increases circulation and calms indigestion. Basil is characterized by having high levels of linalool or fenchol; is primarily used for its antiseptic properties; basil high in methyl chavicol is more anti-inflammatory than antiseptic; and basil with high levels of eugenol has both anti-inflammatory and antiseptic properties. Basil mixed with thyme is used topically as an antiseptic.

Routes of application: Basil can be applied medicinally through inhalation, baths and massage. It has both hot and cold properties and has an invigorating effect. Basil blends well with bergamot, black pepper, cedarwood, Roman chamomile, clary sage, coriander, cypress, eucalyptus, fennel, geranium, ginger, grapefruit, juniper, lavender, lemon, marjoram, niaouli, orange, oregano, palmarosa, pine, rosemary, sage, tea tree and thyme.

Cautions: Basil should not be used for therapeutic purposes in pregnant women; overdoses can cause sudden and severe depression.

Bay (*Pimenta racemosa*)

Beginnings: Roman emperors commonly wore bay laurel leaves (Roman laurel, *Laurus nobilis*) as a sign of wealth and power and to repel evil spirits. Greek priestesses chewed bay leaves for their soporific effect; after meals bay was chewed as a breath freshener.
Historically the bay leaf was distilled with rum in the West Indies, which gave rise to "bay rum," a classic hair tonic and body rub for colds, the flu, bronchitis and muscle aches.

Description: Bay is commonly used as a culinary herb. Bay grows as an evergreen bush, shrub, tree or hedge that can reach 25 feet in height and is characterized by clusters of yellowish-green flowers that bloom in the spring. A spicy, highly aromatic oil is extracted from the leaves and berries; the oil is a yellowish-brown color.

Therapeutic properties: Bay is a general tonic, pulmonary antiseptic, and is commonly used to relieve bronchitis, colds and flu. It can be used to promote healthy digestion and restful sleep. Bay oil can be used topically to relieve rheumatic aches and pains.

Routes of application: Bay is used as an inhalant, and as an additive to bathes and massage. Bay is commonly used in perfumes and exotic bath essences. Bay blends well with bergamot, black pepper, cardamom, cinnamon, clove, coriander, frankincense, geranium, ginger, lavender, grapefruit, lemon, mandarin, nutmeg, orange, petitgrain, rosemary, sandalwood and ylang ylang.

Benzoin (*Styrax benzoin*)

Beginnings: The gum from the benzoin tree was used first in Asia in incense to repel evil spirits. The Arabic name for benzoin, *luban jawi*, means "incense of Java"; European traders shortened the name to banjawi, then later changed it to "Benjamin" and the finally to benzoin. The tincture is used in friar's balsam and as a "fixative" in perfume.

Description: The benzoin tree is cultivated in Borneo, Java, Malaysia, Sumatra and Thailand. Similar to the rubber tree, its gum is extracted from the bark by making a deep incision in the trunk. The gum is dark and is characterized by reddish-brown streaks. The pigments contain oils that produce a vanilla-like aroma.

Therapeutic properties: Benzoin is commonly used for urinary infections. Benzoin has a warming, relaxing property; it is useful as a chest rub for treating bronchitis, coughs and colds. Bezoin is effective for treating skin problems and gout.

Routes of application: Benzoin can be used in inhalants, message oils and in cough medicines. Benzoin produces an energizing oil which can be used in one of two forms; a simple tincture or as a compound (the tincture is the safest form of benzoin).

Bergamot (*Citrus bergamia*)

Beginnings: Bergamot originated in Morocco; its use as an essential oil started in Italy after Christopher Columbus brought bergamot to

Bergamo in northern Italy from the Canary Islands. It was reintroduced to Italy in 1600 from Pergamum, now called Bergama, Turkey. Today, as much as 90% of the world's supply of bergamot is produced in Reggio di Calabria, Italy. It is also a major cash crop of the Ivory Coast, Morocco, Tunisia and Algeria.

Description: The small bergamot tree produces a small, green, bitter fruit is related to the orange tree. The essential oils of bergamot are extracted from the fresh peel of the ripe fruit. The oil is emerald green, smells spicier than lemon oil. Bergamot is used as the flavoring for Earl Grey tea. Key constituents:

Limonene (30-45%)
Linaly Acetate (22-36%)
Linalol (3-15%)
Gamma-Terpinene (6-10%)
Beta-Pinene (5.5-9.5%)

Therapeutic properties: Bergamot has a strong uplifting and refreshing action. It has antiseptic properties and is commonly used for infections of the mouth, sore throat and skin. Bergamot is used to reduce fever and relieve bronchitis and indigestion.

Routes of application: Bergamot mixes well with most essential oils including black pepper, clary sage, cypress, frankincense, geranium, helichrysum, jasmine, lavender, mandarin, nutmeg, orange, ormenis flower, rosemary, sandalwood, vetiver and ylang ylang and is a common additive to perfumes.

Cautions: In concentrations above one percent bergamot can irritate the skin. While bergamot is commonly added to commercial "tanning" products to stimulate the production of melanin, one should never attempt to make their own tanning agents.

Birch (*Betula lenta, B. alleghaniensis*)

Beginnings: The birch tree originates from Scandinavia, Canada and northern Maine. The essential oil of birch is steam distilled from the wood. The North American birch is a large tree with a fragrant inner bark; it is the original source of the "wintergreen" essential oil used for chewing gum, candy and breath mints.

Description: Key constituents:
Methyl salicylate (> 90%)

Therapeutic properties: Birch has analgesic, antispasmodic, anti-inflammatory, liver tonic properties; it is used to relieve arthritis, rheumatism, inflammation, muscular pain, fibromyalgia, tendonitis, cystitis, eczema, acne, urinary infections, gout, gallstones, edema, high blood pressure, osteoporosis and cramps. The active ingredient, methyl salicylate, is similar in action to that of aspirin as an anti-inflammatory and analgesic.

Routes of application: Birch essential oil can be applied to the bottom of the feet or diluted with an extender oil; can be diluted at three to five drops in a Tblsp of bath oil and added to a hand hot bath or used as a massage. Birch oil blends well with basil, cypress, geranium, juniper berries, lavender, lemongrass, marjoram, peppermint and Roman chamomile.

Caution: Pregnant women should consult their physician before use.

Black Pepper (*Piper nigrum*)

Beginnings: Black pepper originated in Madagascar, Egypt and India. Black pepper was used in India over 4,000 years ago. Black pepper was used by the Egyptians in their art of mummification (black pepper was found in the nostrils and abdomen of the mummy of Ramses II). Indian monks ate several black peppercorns each day to maintain their stamina and energy.

Description: Black pepper is a climbing woody vine. The vine clings to trees for support and shade; it is characterized by small white flowers that produce red berries. The essential oils of black pepper are steam distilled from the berries. Key Constituents:

Beta Caryophyllene (25-35%)
Limonene (8-12%)
Sabinene (8-10%)
Alpha and Beta Pinenes (10-15%)

Therapeutic properties: The essential oils of black pepper are used to relieve toothache, as an expectorant, enhances digestion, has analgesic properties and reduces fever.

Routes of application: Black pepper oil is classically applied to the bottom of the feet; massage; add to base oil for safe application. Black pepper oil mixes well with bergamot, clary sage, clove, coriander, cumin, fennel, frankincense, geranium, ginger, grapefruit, juniper, lavender, lemon, lemongrass, lime, mandarin, marjoram, myrrh, orange, nutmeg, palmarosa, patchouli, rosemary, sage, sandalwood, spikenard, tea tree, valerian, vetiver, ylang ylang and other spice oils.

Cautions: If pregnant consult physician before use.

Cajeput (*Melaleuca leucadendra*)

Beginnings: In Malaysia and other Indonesian islands, cajeput was used for respiratory infections, headaches, rheumatism, toothache, skin conditions, throat infections and sore muscles. Cajeput is the Malaysian word for white tree.

Descrition: Key constituents:

Eucalyptol (50-65%)
Alpha-Terpineol (7-13%)
Limonene (3-8%)
Alpha Pinene (1-3%)

Therapeutic properties: Cajeput is traditionally used to relieve arthritis, acne, respiratory infections, asthma, bronchitis, urinary complaints, coughs, cystitis, stiff joints, toothache, hay fever, bursitis, headaches, insect bites, intestinal problems, laryngitis, dysentery, psoriasis, rheumatism, sinusitis, oily skin, sore throat and viral infections.

Routes of application: Inhale, diffuse or rub on the bottom of the feet. Cajeput mixes well with wintergreen/birch, eucalyptus, juniper berries, peppermint.

Caution: Pregnant women should consult their physician before use.

Cardamom (*Ellettaria cardamomum*)

Beginnings: Cardamom is a relative of ginger root; it is a native to the Middle and Far East; it is used traditionally in Turkish coffee and East Indian Chai tea to impart a warm spicy flavor and aroma. East Indians have traditionally considered the cardamom aroma warmly romantic and a potent aphrodisiac. The essential oil was first distilled in 1544 by Valerius Cordus, following a Portuguese explorer's procuring them from the southwest Indian coast.

Description: Perennial rush-like herb with blade-like leaves; it produces small yellow flowers with violet tips that produce a seed-bearing fruit. Key constituents:

Alpha Terpinyl Acetate (45-55%)
1,8 Cineol (Eucalyptol) (16-24%)
Linalol (4-7%)
Linalyl Acetate (3-7%)
Limonene (1-3%)

Therapeutic properties: The oil of cardamom is antiparalytic, antispasmodic, antibacterial, expectorant, anti-infectious and a vermafuge. The oil of cardamom has been used to relieve paralysis, arthritis, rheumatism, cardiac disorders, seizures, spasms, pulmonary disease, indigestion, intestinal maladies and a wide variety of urinary tract inflammations, anorexia, coughs, debility, bad breath, fatigue, headaches, heartburn, nausea, sciatica, dysmenorrheal, insect bites and general infections.

Routes of application: Diffuse, rub on the bottom of the feet, chest, stomach, solar plexus and thighs. The oil of cardamom blends well with bay, bergamot, black pepper, cedarwood, cinnamon, cistus, clove, coriander, fennel, ginger, grapefruit, jasmine, lemon, lemongrass, *Litsea cubeba*, mandarin, neroli, orange, palmarosa, patchouli, petitgrain, rose, sandalwood, vetiver and ylang-ylang.

Caution: Pregnant women should consult their physician before use.

Carnation (*Dianthus caryophyllus*)

Beginnings: This variety of carnation is commonly referred to as "pinks" because of the color of the flowers. The name is thought to have been derived from the fact that the flower was woven into ancient garlands and crowns - hence carnation.

Description: The carnation was first described in Egypt and France. The plant is a perennial herb, with long, narrow, gray-green leaves growing from the stem. The pink flowers have many petals that sport ragged edges. Where the petals join the center of the flower there are dark pink to purple flecks. The essential oils are extracted from the flower heads. It takes 500 kilograms of flowers to make 1 kg of "concrete" that yields 100 grams of carnation absolute. Key constituents:

Eugenol
B-Caryophyllene
Caryophyllene Oxide

Therapeutic properties: Carnation essential oils have calmative, sedative, neurotonic and soporific properties. It is used primarily in aroma-psychology, such as emotional problems, stress, feelings of detachment, overactive mind, inability to communicate, emotional solitude and feelings of neglect.

Routes of application: Carnation blends well with rose maroc, rose otto, cardamom, clary sage, clove, coriander, hyacinth, jasmine, lemon, black pepper, bergamot, lemon, Roman chamomile, orange, neroli, vetiver, ylang ylang and yuzu.

Cedarwood (*Cedrus deodora, C. atlantica, Juniperus virginiana*)

Beginnings: Cedarwood oil, like sandalwood oil, was used by the Egyptians for embalming solutions. Cedarwood was historically and is also currently used as an antiseptic and as an ingredient in cosmetics. The original cedarwood oil came from the Lebanese cedar, however, it now comes from the red cedar. Bible references include: Leviticus 14:4 "*Then shall the priest command to take for him that is to be cleansed two birds alive and clean, and cedarwood, and scarlet, and hyssop.*" Leviticus 14:6 "*As for the living bird, he shall take it, and the cedarwood, and the scarlet, and the hyssop, and shall dip them and the living bird in the blood of the bird (that was) killed over the running water.*" Leviticus 14:49 "*And he shall take to cleanse the house two birds, and cedarwood, and scarlet, and hyssop.*"

Description: The cedarwood tree is an evergreen that grows to 50 to 100 foot tall and can live for more than 1000 years. The cedarwood oil comes primarily from North Africa and the United States. The clear syrup-like oil is steam distilled from cedarwood unfit for furniture manufacturing; the scent of cedarwood oil is the same as the scent from wooden pencils. Key constituents:

Alpha-Himachalene (10-20%)
Beta-Himachalene (35-55%)
Gamma-Himachalene (8-15%)
Delta-Cadinene (2-6%)

Therapeutic properties: Typically cedarwood is used for respiratory problems including bronchitis and catarrh; for skin problems including acne, alopecia, dandruff and eczema; and as a diuretic and urinary disinfectant.

Routes of application: Can be administered as an inhalant and topically as a massage oil; can increase sexual response. Cedarwood oil blends well with bay, bergamot, cardamom, clary sage, cypress, eucalyptus, frankincense, geranium, grapefruit, juniper berries, lavender, marjoram, orange, neroli, palmarosa, petitgrain, rosemary, rose oils, sandalwood and ylang ylang.

Cautions: Pregnant women should contact their physician before use. Cedarwood can produce skin irritation in high concentrations.

Chamomile (*Anthemis nobilis;* German -*Matricaria recutita*)

Beginnings: The Egyptians looked at chamomile as a sacred flower and used it to connect with the sun god. Chamomile was used in various religious ceremonies and used medicinally for seizures and reducing fevers.

Description: Chamomile is found growing wild and is cultivated throughout Europe and North Africa. Chamomile is characterized by fine feathery leaves with small white or yellow-centered daisy-like flowers. The chamomile fragrance is so apple-like, that the Spanish call it manzanilla, or "little apple" and the Greeks refer to it as "earth apples." The pale blue oil is extracted by steam distillation from the flowers and has an apple-like aroma. Chamomile blends well with rose, geranium and lavender oils. Key constituents:

Chamazulene (2-5%)
Bisabolol Oxide A (32-42%)
Trans-Beta-Farnesene (18-26%)
Bisbolol Oxide B (3-6%)
Bisbolone Oxide A (3-6%)
Cis Spiro Ether (4-8%)

Therapeutic properties: Chamomile is prized for its anti-inflammatory and sedative properties. It is typically used for earache, allergies, anemia, burns, dermatitis, diarrhea, fever, indigestion, insomnia, dysmenorrhea, menopause, rheumatism, toothache, inflammation, acne, chilblains, muscle spasms and ulcers.

Routes of application: Chamomile is used as an infusion; the oil can be used orally, in the bath, and as hair preparations. Can be diluted and used for childhood ailments. It blends well with bergamot, Roman chamomile, lavender, cypress, frankincense, geranium, marjoram, lemon, grapefruit, naiouli, patchouli, pine, ravensara, rosemary and tea tree.

Chamomile (Roman) (*Chamaemelum nobile*)

Beginnings: Plant originated in Egypt and Utah. Roman chamomile was used traditionally to relieve skin conditions. For centuries mothers have used chamomile to sedate crying children.

Description: The essential oil of Roman chamomile is steam distilled from the flowers. A very gentle aromatherapy essential oil. Key constituents:

Isobutyl Angelate + Isamyl Methacrylate (30-45%)
Isoamyl Angelate (12-22%)
Methyl Allyl Angelate (6-10%)
Isobutyl n-butyrate (2-9%)
2-Methyl Butyl Angelate (3-7%)

ORAC value (Oxygen Radical Absorbance Capacity) 2,446

Therapeutic properties: Calming for preanesthesia and tension, antispasmodic, anti-inflammatory, antiparasitic, relieve earache, reduce fever, soothe stomach ache and indigestion, relieve toothaches and teething pain, relieves allergies, supports skin regeneration, bruises, cuts, depression, insomnia, muscle tension, restless legs, dermatitis, acne, eczema and rashes.

Routes of application: Diffuse, inhale, massage and apply to feet, ankles and wrists; Roman chamomile blends well with lavender, geranium, lemon, tea tree, eucalyptus, palmarosa, grapefruit, rose, neroli, jasmine, clary sage.

Cinnamon (*Cinnamomum zeylanicum, C. verum*)

Beginnings: Cinnamon oil was mixed with just about all ancient Chinese remedies. Cinnamon is one of the oldest spices known to man; it is mentioned in he Old Testament; and it was used liberally in ancient Greece, Rome and Egypt. The word cinnamon is derived from the Greek word kinnamon which translates to tube or pipe which describes the bark when used as a spice.

Description: Cinnamon is a large, subtropical evergreen tree with a fragrant bark that can be harvested twice a year for 30 years; it is widely grown in the Far East, Asia, the East Indies and China. Cinnamon has a distinct hot pepper-like taste and aroma; the twigs and leaves are distilled to produce a pungent, bitter-sweet aromatic oil; the oil is a dark yellow-brown color; cinnamon oil is oftentimes used in perfumes.
Key constituents:

Trans-Cinnamaldehyde (40-50%)
Eugenol (20-30%)
Beta-Carophyllene (3-8%)
Linalol (3-7%)

ORAC value - 103,448

Therapeutic properties: Cinnamon can be used to relieve fatigue and depression; it is used as a general tonic and as a tonic for the respiratory and digestive systems; the oil is particularly useful for coughs, colds, flu, stomach ache and diarrhea. Cinnamon oil is frequently used as an aphrodisiac and for impotence.

Routes of application: Can be administered as an inhalant or a massage oil. Cinnamon can be burned to prevent the spread of flu virus; cinnamon bark and oils are added to pot pourri; can be used as a massage oil or compress to relieve muscle spasm. It blends well with clove, nutmeg, ylang ylang, mandarin, orange, lemon, grapefruit, *Litsea cubeba*, rose maroc, bay, bergamot, carnation, coriander, cardamom, frankincense, geranium, ginger, lemongrass, marjoram, patchouli, petitgrain and yuzu.

Cautions: Cinnamon should be used as a diluted oil in low concentrations or under professional supervision. Pregnant women should contact their physician before use.

Citronella (*Cymbopogon nardus*)

Beginnings: Citronella originated from Sri Lanka, Philippines and Egypt. Numerous cultures have used citronella oil to eliminate intestinal parasites, relieve digestive and dysmenorrhea, headaches, respiratory infections, neuralgia, fatigue, insomnia, oily skin and used as an insecticide.

Description: This tropical grass releases its strong fragrance when broken or crushed. It was recorded that in 332 B.C., Alexander the Great, while riding an elephant along the Egyptian border "became intoxicated when he inhaled the fragrance of nard (the old name for citronella) as it was crushed under foot." The oil of citronella is steam distilled from the leaves. Key constituents:

Geraniol (18-30%)
Limonene (5-10%)
Trans-Methyl Isoeugenol (4-10%)
Geranyl Acetate (5-10%)
Borneol (3-8%)

Therapeutic properties: Antibacterial, insect-repellent, antifungal, anti-inflammatory, antiseptic, antispasmodic, deodorant and insecticidal. The oil of citronella can be used as an attractant in fish bait, however, a primary use was and is to keep away mosquitoes, ticks, fleas and other insects.

Routes of application: Diffuse, inhale, massage and topical application to the bottom of the feet. Citronella oil blends well with bergamot, cedarwood, geranium, lemon, orange and pine.

Clary Sage (Clear eye) (*Salvia sclarea*)

Beginnings: The name Salvia is taken from the Latin word for "good health." It is used to flavor cheap wines in an effort to give them the taste of Muscatel; it is used in the manufacturing process of vermouths and liqueurs; in Europe it is commonly used as a substitute for hops in fermenting beer; the seeds are used in folk medicine for conditions of the eye - thus the name "clear eye."

Description: Clary sage is a biennial plant that grows up to three feet high; it is characterized by long hairy leaves, it has lilac-pink flowers that sit atop long thin stems. The oil is steam distilled from the flowering tops. Key constituents:

Linalol (7-24%)
Linalyl Acetate (56-78%)
Germacrene D (2-12%)
Sclareol (0.4-3%)
Geranyl Acetate

Therapeutic properties: Clary sage has antiseptic, calmative, tonic, emmenagogue, anti-infectious, antispasmodic, antisudorific, aphrodisiac, nerve tonic, nervine and estrogen-like properties; it is typically used for muscular fatigue, dysmenorrhea, calming, stress, depression, cramps and excessive perspiration.

Routes of application: Diffuse or apply topically to the bottoms of the feet, ankles and wrists. Clary sage blends well with geranium, lemon, grapefruit, lavender, sandalwood, cypress, mandarin, jasmine, juniper, rose, bergamot, bay, black pepper, Roman chamomile, coriander, lime, patchouli, tea tree (it blends well with almost all flower absolutes in small doses).

Cautions: Pregnant women should consult their physician before use.

Clove (*Syzygium aromaticum, Eugenia caryophyllata*)

Beginnings: Clove originated from Madagascar and the Spice Islands. Clove was used in ancient China as a medicine. To fragrance their mouth, courtiers would put clove buds in their mouth when speaking to the emperor. The people on the island of Ternate were free of epidemics until the 16th century when Dutch conquerors invaded the island and destroyed the clove groves cultivated on the island. European doctors historically breathed through clove-filled leather beaks to ward off the plague. It is steam distilled from the buds and small twigs and stems.

Description: Clove buds are the unripe flower buds of a short, slender evergreen tree that bears buds for at least 100 years. Key constituents:

Eugenol (75-87%)
Eugenol Acetate (8-15%)
Beta-Carophyllene (2-7%)

ORAC value 10,786,875

Therapeutic properties: Clove essential oils are highly antimicrobial, antiseptic, analgesic, bactericidal, antioxidant, hemostatic and anti-inflammatory. Historically used as a home remedy and by the dental industry for relieving toothache. According to Dr. Jean Valnet, clove oil can prevent contagious diseases, relieve arthritis, bronchitis, cholera, cystitis, dental infection, amoebic dysentery, diarrhea, tuberculosis, acne, fatigue, thyroid dysfunction, bad breath, headache, hypertension, insect bites, nausea, neuritis, dermatitis, rheumatism, sinusitis, skin cancer, chronic skin disease, bacterial colitis, sores, viral hepatitis, warts and lymphoma.

Route of application: Diffuse, inhale or apply topically diluted with a carrier oil; add one or two drops in four fluid ounces of water and use as a gargle. Apply undiluted to palms of hands, bottom of feet, and on gums and teeth. Blends well with bay, basil, bergamot, cinnamon, clary sage, grapefruit, geranium, grapefruit, ginger, jasmine, lavender, lemon, nutmeg, mandarin, orange, palmarosa, peppermint, Roman chamomile, rose, rosemary and ylang-ylang.

Caution: If pregnant consult physician before use; do not use undiluted clove oil directly on an infant's skin or gums.

Comfrey (Symphytum officinale)

Beginnings: Comfrey was a favorite of Nicholas Culpepper, the 17th century English herbalist - "Comfrey helpeth those that spit blood or maketh a bloody urine." The root was boiled in water or wine and the extract consumed for all kinds of internal maladies, "ulcers of the lungs" and increase blood flow.

Description: Comfrey commonly grows wild along wet or swampy waterways. Comfrey is characterized by hairy and fleshy leaves that can irritate the skin of susceptible individuals. The stem grows to three feet in height and displays a purplish flower. The leaves and roots are used in herbal decoctions, while the oil is extracted from the stalks and leaves.

Therapeutic properties: Comfrey contains allantoin, a phytochemical that can stimulate cell repair following injuries; comfrey oil is of particular use for the treatment of wounds and skin disorders including eczema, psoriasis, stretch marks, dysmenorrhea and menopausal symptoms.

Routes of application: Massage oils and compresses.

Coriander (*Coriandrum sativum*)

Beginnings: The coriander plant originated in Russia and India. Coriander seeds were found in the ancient Egyptian tombs of Ramses II and Tutankhamun. Coriander seeds are used to flavor Chartreuse and Benedictine liqueurs that are produced by French monks.

Description: Coriander oil is steam distilled from the seeds. Key constituents:

Linalol (65-78%)
Alpha-Pinene (3-7%)
Camphor (4-6%)
Gamma-Terpinene (2-7%)
Limonene (2-5%)

Geranyl Acetate (1-3.5%)
Geraniol (0.5-3%)

Therapeutic properties: Coriander oil is used to relieve arthritis, diarrhea, respiratory infections, indigestion, digestive spasms, poor circulation, diabetes, supports pancreatic function, rheumatism, gout, infections, measles, headaches, nausea, muscular aches, pain, neuralgia, acne, psoriasis, dermatitis, PMS and stress.

Routes of application: Primarily applied topically; it blends well with bergamot, clary sage, black pepper, cardamom, cinnamon, clove, cypress, frankincense, geranium, ginger, grapefruit, jasmine, lemon, neroli, nutmeg, orange, palmarosa, petitgrain, pine, ravensara, sandalwood, vetiver and ylang ylang.

Caution: Coriander oil can be strongly sedative. If pregnant consult physician before use.

Cypress (*Cupressus sempervirens*)

Beginnings: Egyptians used cypress oil for medicinal purposes and the wood to decorate their stone coffins. The tree gave its name to the island of Cyprus. The cross of Jesus is believed to have been made of cypress. The French traditionally plant the trees in grave yards.

Description: A tall conical evergreen tree that originated in Asia, and became commonly grown throughout the Mediterranean, including Algeria and France. The essence is made by distilling the leaves, twigs and cones of the tree. The oil is clear and pale yellow or green; it has a spicy and refreshing fragrance similar to pine needles. Key constituents:
Alpha-Pinene (40-65%)
Beta-Pinene (0.5-3%)
Delta-3-Carene (12-25%)
Limonene (1.8-5%)
Cedrol (0.8-7%)
Myrcene (1-3.5%)

Manoyle Oxide
Iso-pimaradiene
Karahanaenone

Therapeutic properties: Cypress is highly regarded for its astringent and antiseptic properties. Cypress oil is commonly used as a sedative, muscular tonic, for circulatory problems, colds, coughs, flu, hemorrhoids, varicose veins, whooping cough, dysmenorrhea and menopausal problems. It is often used as an astringent for oily skin.

Routes of application: Massage, bath and inhalation are common routes of administration. Cypress oil can be used as a compress for swelling or rheumatism. It blends well with bergamot, cedarwood, clary sage, eucalyptus, frankincense, geranium, jasmine, lemon, lavender, orange, lime, pine, mandarin, marjoram, ravensara, Roman chamomile, rosemary, sandalwood and tea tree.

Cautions: Cypress oil should not be used for people who suffer from hypertension.

Eucalyptus (*Eucalyptus globulus*)

Beginnings: Eucalyptus is one of the tallest trees in the world. The tree originated in Australia and transplanted to Tasmania, China, United States, Brazil and the Mediterranean. There are about 200 or more species of eucalyptus trees. The Australian Aborigines are considered to be the first people to use eucalyptus oil medicinally. Eucalyptus oil was first distilled in Australia in 1788 by the Surgeon General of the colony, Dr. John White. The tree is fast growing and requires large volumes of water which has allowed it to convert swamp land into usable farm land. Because this process eliminated the breeding ground of the malaria mosquito, the trees took on the reputation during the 1800s of eliminating "miasma" or "fever" when the etiology and epidemiology of malaria was not yet known. Thus the name - "fever tree."

Description: The silvery, pale blue-green leaves produce a pale yellow oil. The oil has a cool camphorous aroma. The fresh leaves produce a high yield of a highly potent oil that is used widely in aroma therapy programs. Key constituents:

1,8 Cineole (58-80%)
Alpha Pinene (10-22%)
Limonene (1-8%)
Para-Cymene (1-5%)
Trans-Pinocarveol (1-5%)
Aromadendrene (1-5%)
Globulol (0.5-1.5%)

ORAC value 24,157

Therapeutic properties: The primary constituent of eucalyptus oil is the highly antiseptic eucalyptol. The oil is highly regarded for use in asthma, bronchitis, flu, sinusitis, clear a stuffy head, cystitis, skin infections, rheumatism and sores; it is also used to reduce fever and as a diuretic.

Routes of application: Baths, diffuse, inhalation, humidifier, rubs and massages. The oil has a general cooling effect on the body. Eucalyptus oil blends well with cypress, geranium, German chamomile, ginger, grapefruit, juniper, lavender, lemon, lemongrass, melissa, peppermint, pine, Roman chamomile, rosemary, sandalwood and thyme.

Caution: Do not take internally; if pregnant consult with physician.

Fennel (*Foeniculum vulgare*)

Beginnings: Ancient Greeks and Romans used fennel seeds to give them strength and long life, repel evil spirits, kill fleas and freshen their breath. Pliny lists 22 remedies that contained fennel. The Greek name for fennel was marathrion (derived from maraino) which translates to "to grow thin."

Description: Fennel is a perennial/biennial European plant that grows by the sea; they have delicate bright green feathery leaves; there are tufts of yellow flowers; it is often referred to as "licorice" plant or anise because it tastes and smells like licorice. The oil is steam distilled from crushed seeds. The fresh leaves are used as a culinary herb for fish dishes; fennel seeds, which smell and taste like anis seed are used in the making of licorice. Key constituents:

Trans-Anethol (60-80%)
Fenchone + Linalol (12-16%)
Alpha-Pinene (3-5%)
Methyl Chavicol (2-5%)

Therapeutic properties: Fennel seeds are used as a diuretic and a laxative; they have estrogen-like properties; they are used in the treatment of colic, constipation, indigestion, kidney stones, menopausal symptoms, nausea and obesity. It is used as a carminative, emmenagogue, phyto-estrogen, galactagogue, depurative, diuretic, stimulant, regenerative, anti-spasmodic, antiseptic, antibiotic, vermafuge and expectorant. Fennel seeds can be used to increase milk production for breastfeeding.

Routes of application: Massage, the oil is used for indigestion and flatulence; it is an ingredient of gripe water and is commonly defused as a tea. Fennel blends well with juniper, geranium, lavender, bergamot, black pepper, cardamom, cypress, ginger, grapefruit, lemon, marjoram, niaouli, pine, ravensara, rosemary, sandalwood and ylang-ylang.

Cautions: People with seizure disorders and estrogen sensitive cancer should avoid the use of fennel oil; pregnant women should consult their physician before use.

Frankincense (*Boswellia thurifera*)

Beginnings: Frankincense (also known as olibanum) and myrrh were the first tree resins used as incense by the Egyptians. They were burned to cleanse the air of sick rooms and during religious ceremonies to fend off evil spirits. Frankincense and myrrh were considered to be as valuable as gem stones. Frank incense and myrrh were given as gifts to the Christ child by the three Magi or Wise Men. The Christ child was born in a barn filled with animal manure, animal urine, flies and animals. The child mortality rate was very high 2000 years ago and the choice of the anti-bacterial and the anti-viral resins of frankincense and myrrh were the perfect and appropriate gifts. The resin comes from a small tree grown in Arabia, Africa and China. It was first brought to Europe in the late 17th century.

Description: To harvest the resin, a deep cut is made into the tree trunk, the resin flows from the bark and forms into teardrop shaped nuggets that harden on contact with the air. The oil is spicy with camphor tones that become lemon-like when mixed with myrrh. Key constituents:

Alpha-Pinene (28-49%)
Limonene (10-16%)
Sabinene (3-7%)
Myrcene (8-12%)
Beta Caryophyllene (3-7%)
Alpha Thuyene (4-8%)
Paracymene (2-5%)

Therapeutic properties: The aroma has an uplifting effect with enhancement of concentration; it acts as an expectorant and is useful for bronchitis, coughs, colds, and laryngitis; frankincense is used as an astringent for the skin and is thought to reduce wrinkles.

Routes of application: Inhalation, baths and massage. Inhale to loosen catarrh or relax with several drops in the bath. It blends well with basil, bergamot, clary sage, cypress, geranium, grapefruit, lavender, lemon, orange, mandarin, myrrh, neroli, palmarosa, patchouli, pine, rose maroc, rose otto, sandalwood, vetiver and ylang-ylang.

Geranium (*Pelargonium adorantissimum, P. graveoloens*)

Beginnings: The geranium originated in Africa and was not brought to Europe until 1690. It was used in the ancient days for tumors, burns and wounds.

Description: Geranium plants are widely cultivated through Europe; the plant grows to two feet in height. There are 700 species of geranium, most of which are grown for their flowers. The pelargoniums in particular produce a rich lemony and sweet yellow-green essential oil. The oil is distilled from the leaves, stalks and flowers. Key constituents:

Citronellol + Nerol (35-50%)
Citronnellyl Formate (9-15%)
Geraniol (5-10%)
6,9-Guaiadene (4-8%)
Isomenthone (4-8%)

Therapeutic properties: Geranium oils are used for relieving tension and depression; antispasmodic, stimulates adrenal, anti-tumor, astringent, hemostatic, antibacterial, antifungal, supports skin health, they are used for chilblains, circulatory problems and superficial wounds.

Routes of application: Geranium is used frequently in the perfume industry; as an essential oil, it can be used as a massage and inhaled. Geranium blends well with all other oils, including lemon, grapefruit, lavender, rosemary, Roman chamomile, peppermint, clove, clary sage, ginger, palmarosa, ylang ylang, sandalwood, mandarin, juniper, cypress, bergamot, black pepper, fennel, frankincense, orange, rose maroc, rose otto and jasmine.

Caution: If pregnant consult physician.

Ginger (*Zingiber officinale*)

Beginnings: The ginger plant was originally native to China. Ginger was historically used to combat the effects of motion sickness and has been revered for its gentle stimulating effect. Women in the West African country of Senegal weave belts of ginger root fiber to restore their impotent mate's sexual prowess. It is used to make ginger ale, ginger beer, ginger wine and ginger candy.

Description: The ginger plant is a perennial herb growing to more than four feet high. Long lance-shaped leaves protrude from a central stem; the yellow flowers grow from the top of the stalk. Ginger essential oils are steam distilled from the roots. Digestive tonic, sexual tonic, reduces pain and expectorant. Key constituents:

Zingibene + Alpha-Selinene (25-40%)
Beta-Sesquiphellandrene + Delta-Cadinene (7-14%)
Beta-Phellandrena + 1,8 Cineol + Limonene (8-15%)
AR Curcumene (5-11%)

Therapeutic properties: Ginger root is traditionally used to relieve arthritis, rheumatism, indigestion, digestive disorders, motion sickness, alcoholism, loss of appetite, chills, respiratory infections, congestion, coughs, muscular aches and pains, nausea, sinusitis, sore throats and sprains.

Routes of application: Diffuse or apply topically. Ginger root or the essential oils are commonly added to food. Ginger essential oils mix well with all spice oils, bergamot, cedarwood, all citrus oils, clove, coriander, *Eucalyptus radiata*, frankincense, geranium, grapefruit, jasmine, juniper, lemon, lime, mandarin, myrtle, neroli, palmarosa, patchouli, rose maroc, rosemary, sandalwood, spearmint, vetiver and ylang-ylang.

Caution: Pregnant women should consult their physician before use; avoid direct sun exposure after use; repeated use can produce contact sensitivity on skin.

Goldenrod (*Solidago canadensis*)

Beginnings: Goldenrod originated in Canada. The genus name, Solidago, is derived from the Latin solide, which translates to "to make whole." During the Boston Tea Party, after English tea was thrown into the harbor, American colonist drank goldenrod tea, which they called "Liberty Tea."

Description: Goldenrod oils are steam distilled. The general action is diuretic, anti-inflammatory, liver tonic, macrolytic, stimulant and tonic. Key constituents:

Germacrene D (22-35%0
Alpha-Pinene (10-18%)
Myrcene (8-15%)
Sabinene (5-11%)
Limonene (6-12%)

Therapeutic properties: Goldenrod oil helps to thin mucus secretions, asthma, relieves candida infestations and relieves congested mucus; it promotes urination, cleans out the kidney, relieves hypertension, reduces inflammation and reduces the risk of infection.

Routes of application: Diffuse or apply topically; can be used as a wash or compress for wounds, headaches, arthritis and rheumatism, as a gargle, sore throat, laryngitis and thrush.

Grapefruit (*Citrus paradise*)

Beginnings: The grapefruit tree was introduced into the West Indies from China by a Captain Shaddock and the fruit was locally known as the "Shaddoc" fruit. In 1809 the seeds traveled with Spanish settlers to the United States, however, it was not grown commercially until 1880. Grapefruit is now grown in the USA, South Africa, Israel and Brazil and is actually a hybrid between C. *maxima and* C. *sinensis.*

Description: Grapefruit oils are mechanically cold pressed from the fresh skin. Key constituents:

Limonene (88-95%)
Myrcene (1-4%)

Therapeutic properties: Grapefruit oil is antiseptic, disinfectant, detoxifying and diuretic, fat-dissolving properties, skin cleansing for oily skin, antidepressant, emotionally uplifting, agent for drug withdrawal, eating disorders, fatigue, jet lag, liver disorders, migraine headaches, PMS, stress and cleansing effect on the lymphatic and vascular system.

Routes of application: Diffuse, apply topically and take orally. Grapefruit oil mixes well with essential oils of basil, bergamot, cedarwood, chamomile, cypress, frankincense, geranium, juniper, lavender, peppermint, rosemary, rosewood and ylang-ylang.

Caution: Pregnant women should consult physician before use.

Helichrysum (*Helichrysm italicum, H. angustifolium*)

Beginnings: Helichrysum originated in France, Hungary, Yugoslavia and Corsica. Helichrysum has been used to encourage regeneration of tissue and nerves, improving circulation and various skin conditions. This everlasting flower is also called everlast and immortelle.

Description: Helichrysum is an evergreen herb that reaches 20 inches in height, it has long stems, off of which grow many thin, needle-like, velvety leaflets. At the top of each stem is a clump of about 30 tiny flower heads that are covered in bright yellow scales. There are more than 500 varieties of helichrysum; the oil is extracted from the flowers by steam distillation. Key Constituents:

Neryl Acetate (25-35%)
Gamma Curcuneme (9-15%)
Limonene (8-13%)
Neryl Propionate (3-7%)
Alpha Pinene (3-8%)
Beta-Caryophyllene (1-5%)
Linalol (1-4%)
Nerol (2-5%)

ORAC value 17,420

Therapeutic properties: The essential oil of helichrysum has anticoagulant, anesthetic, dissolves hematomas, mucolytic, expectorant and antispasmodic properties; it stimulates the liver, reduces scar tissue and skin pigments; it balances blood pressure and detoxifies chemicals and various toxins from the body; stems bleeding, relieves hearing loss, pain, arteriosclerosis, atherosclerosis, hypertension, congestive heart failure, cardiac arrhythmias, thrombosis, embolism, liver disorders, phlebitis, sciatica, sinus infection and skin disorders including eczema, dermatitis and psoriasis.

Routes of application: Diffuse and apply topically around outside of ear, temple, forehead, back of neck or affected area. It blends well with bergamot, black pepper, cedarwood, German chamomile, clary sage, cypress, frankincense, geranium, grapefruit, juniper, lavender, lemon, mandarin, naiouli, oregano, palmarosa, ravensara, pine, rosemary, sage, tea tree, thyme, rose maroc, rose otto, ylang-ylang, vetiver and eucalyptus.

Caution: Pregnant women should consult with their physician.

Hyacinth (*Hyacinthus orientalis*)

Beginnings: Named by Linnaeus after Hyacinthus, a Spartan youth beloved by Apollo and Zephyrus. In modern times the countries of origin are Holland, France and Egypt.

Description: It is a perennial herbaceous bulbous plant, with narrow, slender light to dark green leaves and large flower heads with bell shaped white, pink or blue flowers. Key constituents:

Benzyl alcohol
Troxo cinnamly alcohol
Benzaldehyde
Phenylethyl-Alcohol

Therapeutic properties: It has powerful hypnotic, sedative, antidepressant and antiseptic properties. It is used in aroma-psychology, emotional crisis, as a sedative, to relieve stress and tension, calming, mental fatigue, sorrow and feelings of distress.

Routes of application: It blends well with rose maroc, rose otto, lemon, bergamot, grapefruit, *Litsea cubeba*, neroli, ylang-ylang, frankincense, orange, cypress, sandalwood, petitgrain and geranium.

Hyssop (*Hyssopus officinalis*)

Beginnings: Hyssop is mentioned as part of sacrifice ceremonies in the Old Testament. Ancient alchemist used the powdered leaves and roots as a vermafuge. Small quantities were mixed with honey or crushed figs as a mild laxative.

Description: The essential oil is extracted from the leaves and flowers; it is used in perfumes and liqueurs (i.e. - Chartreuse). The plant is characterized by long stalks and blue flowers. Key constituents:

Beta Pinene (13.5-23%)
Sabinene (2-3%)
Pinochamphone (5.5-17.5%)
Iso-Pinochamphone (34.5-50%)
Gemacrene D (2-3%)
Limonene (1-4%)

Therapeutic properties: Hyssop is typically used for skin disorders, supporting the cardiovascular system, including blood pressure problems; bronchitis, coughs and colds.

Routes of application: Hyssop oil is applied through massage and inhalation; it is commonly mixed with cough syrups.

Cautions: Do not use during pregnancy; use only small amounts.

Jasmine (*Jasminum officinale, J. grandiflorum*)

Beginnings: Used commonly by Arabs, Indians and Chinese as perfume and for scenting tea. Jasmine was brought to Europe from Iran in the 16th century. The 17th century herbalist Nicholas Culpeper recommended rubbing the essential oil into "hard contracted limbs to ease muscle cramps." Jasmine has been nicknamed "queen of the night" and "moonlight of the grove."

Description: The *Jasminum grandiflora* species is a small bush that originated in the East Indies and Egypt; it is grown in southern France, Spain, Algeria, Morocco, India and Egypt. Jasmine produces tiny white flowers with a "honey-sweet" floral bouquet with fruity undertones. A deep red essential oil is produced by enfleurage; the essential oil is one of the more expensive ingredients of the perfume industry - the production of one pound of jasmine oil requires 1,000 pounds (3.6 million unpacked jasmine flowers) of jasmine blossoms. Key constituents:

Benzyl Acetate (18-28%)
Benzyl Benzoate (14-21%)
Linalol (3-8%)
Phytol (6-12%)
Isophytol (3-7%)
Squalene (3-7%)

Therapeutic properties: Jasmine is commonly used as a mood enhancer for individuals with anxiety and depression; it is used as an aphrodisiac for both frigidity and impotence; it is used for dysmenorrhea.

Routes of applications: Inhalation, bath and massage will all produce the warming and relaxing properties of jasmine. It blends well with bay, rose maroc, rose otto, neroli, sandalwood, palmarosa, geranium, lemon, clove, grapefruit, clary sage, bergamot, mandarin, orange, patchouli, petitgrain, ylang-ylang, coriander and ginger.

Juniper (*Juniperus communis*)

Beginnings: Grown in North America, Asia, Africa and Europe; juniper is a small shrub with aromatic needles and berries; it was burned as an incense for religious ceremonies and to "ward off the plague" and small pox. The juniper berries are used in the manufacturing process of gin. Bible references include: Job 30:45 "*Who cut up mallows by the bushes, and juniper roots for their meat.*"

Description: Juniper is an evergreen bush with rough thick branches, needle-like leaves, small yellow flowers and bluish-purple berries. The pale yellow essential oil is distilled from the berries (a different essence is obtained from the twigs - cade oil, which is used in veterinary medicine). Key constituents:

Alpha-pinene (20-40%)
Sabinene (3-18%)
Myrcene (1-6%)
Camphor (10-18%)
Limonene (3-8%)
Bornyl Acetate (12-20%)
Terpinene-4-ol (3-8%)

ORAC value 2,517

Therapeutic properties: Juniper is used as an antiseptic, astringent, digestive stimulant, diuretic and a urinary antiseptic including for cystitis, acne, colic, coughs, dermatitis, eczema, flatulence, rheumatism, promotes excretion of uric acid and the healing of skin ulcers. It blends well with rosemary, geranium, lavender, lemon, grapefruit, sandalwood, cypress, clary sage, pine, frankincense, vetiver, cedarwood, sage, mandarin, eucalyptus, bergamot, fennel and rose otto.

Routes of application: Inhalation, baths and massage.

Labrador tea (Ledum) (*Ledum groenlandicum*)

Beginnings: Labrador tea is a plant native of North America; it is a strongly aromatic herb that has been used for centuries as a home remedy. The native peoples of Eastern Canada used this herb for a tea, as a general tonic and to relieve a wide range of kidney diseases. Labrador tea has been used by the Native American people to prevent and cure scurvy for more than 5,000 years. The Cree nation uses Labrador tea to reduce fevers and relieve cold symptoms.

Description: Labrador tea is a plant native of North America; the oil is steam distilled from the leaves. Key constituents:

Limonene (20-35%)
Cis- and Trans-Paramenth 1(7) 8 Diene 8-ol (12-17%)
Cis- and Trans-Paramenthatriene 1,3,8 (8-15%)

Therapeutic properties: Anti-inflammatory, antitumoral, relieves insomnia, relieves prostate infection and congestion, antibacterial, diuretic, hepatoprotectant, hepatitis, cirrhosis, fatty liver, cough, flu, hoarseness and decongestant.

Routes of application: Diffuse or apply topically diluted one drop to one teaspoon of carrier oil.

Lavender (*Lavendula officinalis, L. angustifolia*)

Beginnings: The name lavender is derived from the Roman lavera and the Latin lavandus, which is translated "to wash." Lavender was a revered essential oil that the Romans used in their daily baths; the Romans and the Greeks burned lavender sprigs to perfume their dwellings as well as to defend against the plague. Lavender was introduced into Europe by the Romans. Historically it was used as an antidote against the bites of the funnel web spider, black widow spider and certain snakes (i.e. - vipers and adders).

Description: Lavender is a woody herb that sports long narrow leaves; as the name implies lavender is characterized by purple-blue "lavender" flowers on tall spikes. The lavender oils are steam-distilled from the dried plant; the oil is clear to pale yellow in color with a strong aroma. Key constituents:

Linalyl Acetate (24-45%)
Linalol (25-38%)
Cis-beta-Ocimene (4-10%)

Trans-beta- Ocimene (1.5-6%)
Terpinene-4-ol (2-6%)

ORAC value 3,669

Therapeutic properties: Lavender has sedative and tonic effects; it is used to "balance" the nervous system, insomnia, migraines, it is antiseptic, skin conditions including acne, stretch marks, burns, sun burn, dandruff, hair loss, infections of the respiratory system, digestive tract, reduces hypertension, PMS, menopausal symptoms, nausea, phlebitis and the urinary system. Lavender oil can be used to cleanse and disinfect cuts, bruises and skin irritations.

Routes of application: Lavender can be applied through inhalation, baths, room dispersers and massage. Cold wraps, warm towel wraps applied to the chest or forehead can be used as a soothing relaxation to end a long stressful day. It blends well with Roman chamomile, German chamomile, lemon, geranium, eucalyptus, thyme, rosemary, tea tree, peppermint, grapefruit, clary sage, palmarosa, mandarin, juniper, cypress, pine, black pepper, marjoram, cedarwood, bergamot, lemongrass and ravensara.

Lemon (*Citrus limonum*)

Beginnings: The name lemon is derived from the Persian or Arabic, limun, which is thought to have come from the Indian Sanskrit. The lemon tree is thought to have come from the northeast of India and brought to Europe through Arabia. The tree was introduced into California in 1887. Lemons were used by early British sailors to prevent scurvy, purify the ships drinking water and as an antiseptic to clean wounds, bruises and insect bites.

Description: The lemon fruit grows on a classic citrus tree which has whitish-pink blossoms and bright yellow fruit the size of a hen's egg. Lemon is grown in orchards in just about all Mediterranean countries, Brazil, the United States, Argentina, Israel and Africa. The pale yellow essential oil is mechanically expressed from the skin (petitgrain essential oil is derived from small spines on the branches of the lemon tree). The lemon essential oil is used in perfumes; the oil can have a short shelf life and will deteriorate if not stored properly. Key constituents:

Limonene (59 -73%)
Gamma-Terpinene 96-12%)
Beta-Pinene (7-16%)
Alpha-Pinene (1.5-3%)
Sabinene (1.5-3%)

Therapeutic properties: Lemon oil is astringent and antiseptic and is typically used to cleanse and disinfect the skin, boils, shingles, herpes and warts; it can be used for reducing elevated blood pressure, colds, indigestion, fever, asthma, anemia, parasites, malaria, sore throat, varicose veins and gallstones. The vaporized essential oils of lemon can kill *M*eningococcus bacteria in 15 minutes, typhoid bacilli in one hour, *Staphylococcus aureus* in two hours and Pneumococcus bacteria within three hours. Even a 0.2% solution of lemon oil can kill diphtheria bacteria in 20 minutes and inactivate tuberculosis bacteria.

Routes of application: Inhalation, diffuse, baths and massage are typical methods of delivery. Lemon oil combines well with all essential oils including chamomile, *Eucalyptus radiata*, fennel, frankincense, geranium, juniper berries, peppermint, sandalwood and ylang-ylang.

Lemongrass (*Cymbopogon citratus*)

Beginnings: A sweet scented grass that was initially used as an insect repellant and to season food in India, Africa, the Seychelles, Indonesia and Sri Lanka.

Description: lemongrass is a tall-stemmed, grass-like tropical plant growing to four feet in height. Its essential oil is steam-distilled from fresh cut grass and has a lemon-like aroma that is prized for "citrus" soaps, perfumes and skin cleansers. Citral, a primary constituent of lemongrass, is a cleansing antiseptic, deodorant and the dried grass was burned to "clear the mind." Key constituents:

- Citral
- Citronellal
- N-Decylic Aldehyde
- Dipentene
- Farucsol
- Geranial (35-45%)
- Geraniol (5-10%)
- Neral (25-40%)
- Trans-beta-Caryophyllene (2-6%0

ORAC value 17,765

Therapeutic properties: Lemongrass oil is typically used for skin conditions, sore throats, athlete's foot, cardiac tonic, digestive support, insect repellant, respiratory conditions (colds, coughs, bronchitis) and headache.

Routes of application: Typically lemongrass oil is applied via inhalation and massage; lemongrass oil blends well with basil, bergamot, black pepper, cedarwood, clary sage, coriander, cypress, fennel, geranium, ginger, grapefruit, lavender, lemon, marjoram, orange, patchouli, palmarosa, rosemary, tea tree, thyme linalol, vetiver, ylang ylang.

Litsea Cubeba (May-Chang Oil) (*Litsea citrate*)

Beginnings: The countries of origin include China and Java. The name cubeba comes from the small round fruit that resemble those on the climbing shrub *Piper cubeba*, a native plant of Java.

Description: Litsea is a shrub-like tree reaching 30 feet in height; it belongs to the laurel family; slender branches produce lance-shaped leaves, white flowers and small green fruit the size of a peppercorn. The oil; is steam distilled from the ripe fruit. Key constituents:

- Citral

Neral
Geranial
Linalool

Therapeutic properties: Litsea is used as a calmative, anti-infectious, antibiotic, stimulant, vulnerary, antiseptic, stomachic and antidepressant. It is used therapeutically for nervousness, a general tonic, relaxing skin care, acne, indigestion, depression, anxiety, stress, poor appetite, anorexia, cleansing, tissue toning and for eliminating cellulite.

Routes of application: It blends well with bay, basil, black pepper, cardamom, cedarwood, clary sage, coriander, cypress, *Eucalyptus citriodora, Eucalyptus radiata,* frankincense, geranium, ginger, grapefruit, juniper, marjoram, orange, patchouli, palmarosa, petitgrain, Roman chamomile, rosemary, sandalwood, tea tree, thyme, vetiver and ylang-ylang.

Mandarin (*Citrus reticulata*)

Beginnings: The Mandarin orange originated in China, Madagascar and Italy - the fruit was a traditional part of the northern Chinese diet, especially a favorite with the aristocracy.

Description: The plant is a small evergreen tree with white, highly scented flowers that produce a small flattened-round, loose-skinned orange fruit. The essential oil is mechanically extracted by the cold press method from the fresh skin of the fruit. Key constituents:

Citral
Citronellal
Limonene (65-75%)
Gamma-Terpinene (16-22%)
Geraniol
Alpha-Pinene (2-3%)
Beta-Pinene (1.2-2%)
Myrcene (1.5-2%)

Therapeutic properties: The essential oil of Mandarin acts as a weak antispasmodic, digestive tonic, antiseptic, antifungal, stimulates the gallbladder, acne, digestive problems, edema, insomnia, intestinal problems, oily skin, scars, liver spots, age spots, tones the skin, stretch marks, relieves nervous tension and restlessness.

Route of application: Diffuse and can be applied topically. Mandarin essential oil blends well with basil, black pepper, cinnamon, clove, frankincense, jasmine, juniper, lavender, myrrh, neroli, nutmeg, palmarosa, patchouli, petitgrain, citrus oils, Roman chamomile, sandalwood, ylang-ylang and spice oils.

Caution: Pregnant women should consult their physician before using Mandarin oil. Do not use on skin before exposure to the sun.

Manuka (*Leptospermum scoparium*)

Beginnings: All parts of the manuka plant have been used by the Maori people from New Zealand as an important part of their folk medicine. When Captain Cook and his crew landed in New Zealand, they used the manuka leaves for making tea. Cook wrote in his ship's log, "It has a very agreeable bitter taste and flavor when (the leaves) are recent but losses some of both when they are dried." Cook's men learned that if they brewed the tea too strong, it caused them to regurgitate. Manuka was the original "tea tree."

Description: The manuka plant is a narrow shrub or small tree with a rich red wood; small, dark, pointed, concave leaves; and small pink or red flowers. The essential oil is steam distilled from the leaves and branch tips. Key constituents:

Beta-Caryphyllen
Geraniol
Geranial
Linalol
Alpha-Pinene

Geranuylacetate

Therapeutic properties: Manuka essential oil has antibiotic, antifungal, antiseptic, anti-infectious, analgesic and vulnerary properties; and it is used to treat athlete's foot, ringworm, thrush, skin infections, colds, flu, sore throat, rheumatism, muscular pain, urinary infections, intestinal infections, burns and wounds.

Route of application: Blends well with basil, bergamot, black pepper, Roman chamomile, German chamomile, clary sage, cypress, eucalyptus, geranium, grapefruit, lavender, lemon, marjoram, orange, patchouli, peppermint, petitgrain, pine, ravensara, rosemary, sage, sandalwood, tea tree, thyme, *Litsea cubeba* and yuzu.

Marjoram (*Origanum marjorana, Majorana hortensis*)

Beginnings: The Greeks cultivated marjoram for their perfumes and medicinal herbal preparations. Marjoram was known as the "herb of happiness" to the Romans and "Joy of the Mountains" to the Greeks. It was grown as a potted plant by the ancient Egyptians; it was used in unguents and perfumes. Greek women used oils infused with marjoram on their heads as a relaxant. It was used in 16th century Europe, on the floors of rooms to produce a pleasant odor as you walked.

Description: A widely used culinary herb that is now grown world-wide. The amber essential oil is steam-distilled from the fresh and dried leaves and flowers; its "warm and spicy" oil is commonly used in male fragrances. Key constituents:

Terpinene-4-ol (25-35%)
Gamma-Terpinene (12-20%)
Linalol +Cis-4-Thujanol (3-8%)
Alpha-Terpinene (6-13%)
Alpha-Terpineol (2-6%)
Sabinene (2-6%)

Therapeutic properties: The essential oil is a warming agent that is used to relieve muscle spasm and cramps, anxiety, insomnia, arthritis, rheumatism, antibacterial, asthma, bronchitis, respiratory infections, fungal and viral infections, ringworm, shingles, circulatory conditions, regulates blood pressure and edema, constipation, headaches, anxiety, dysmenorrhea, muscular strains, bruises, burns, sunburn, cuts, neuralgia and as a nerve tonic.

Routes of application: Inhalation and massage; it blends well with bergamot, lavender and rosemary. Marjoram oil can be steam-inhaled and rubbed into the sinuses and temples; it blends well with Bergamot, cedarwood, chamomile, cypress, lavender, nutmeg, orange, rosemary, rosewood and ylang-ylang.

Cautions: Do not use marjoram oil in the first trimester of pregnancy. High doses of the oil can produce a narcotic-like depressing effect, including a sexual depressant.

Melaleuca alternifolia (*Melaleuca alternifolia*)

Beginnings: The legendary melaleuca tree originated in Australia. The essential oil of melaleuca (Tea tree oil) is steam distilled from the leaves. The antibacterial, antimicrobial and antiseptic properties of the essential oils were discovered by the Aboriginal people of Australia.

Description: Key constituents:

Gama Terpinene (10-28%)
Alpha-Terpinene (5-13%)
1,8 Cineole (Eucalyptol) (0-15%)
Alpha-Terpineol (1.5-8%)
Para-Cymene (0.5-12%)
Terpinenol-4 (30-45%)
Limonene (0.5-4%)
Aromadendrene (trace-7%)
Delta-Cadinene (trace-8%)
Alpha Pinene (1-6%)

Monoterpenes: alpha pinene, beta-pinene, myrcene; Sesquiterpenes; Monoterpene alcohols (45-50%); Terpene oxides.

Therapeutic properties: Anti-infection, antibacterial (active against wide spectrum of gram positive and gram negative bacteria), antifungal, antiviral, antiparasitic, antiseptic, anti-inflammatory, immunostimulant, cardiotonic, venous decongestant, relieves phlebitis, neurotonic, analgesic, athlete's foot, bronchitis, respiratory infections, gingivitis, receding gums, pyorrhea, skin problems (acne, burns, candida, cold sores, shingles, ingrown toenails, warts and wounds), sore throat, sunburn, tonsillitis and vaginal yeast infections.

Routes of application: Diffuse or apply topically. Melaleuca oils blend well with all citrus oils, cypress, *Eucalyptus radiata*, *E. globulus*, clary sage, juniper, pine, marjoram, oregano, peppermint, ravensara, thyme. lavender, rosemary, basil, bergamot, black pepper, Roman chamomile, German chamomile, thyme.

Caution: Pregnant women should consult their physician before use.

Melaleuca ericifolia (*Melaleuca ericifolia; a.k.a. Australian Rosalina*)

Beginnings: The *Melaleuca ericifolia* tree originated in Australia.

Description: Key constituents:

Alpha-Pinene (5-10%)
1,8 Cineol + Beta Phellandrene (18-28%)
Alpha-Terpineol (1-5%)
Para-Cymene (1-6%)
Linalol (34-45%)
Aromadendrene (2-6%)

Therapeutic properties: Relieves respiratory diseases (bronchitis, asthma, colds, etc.), cynitis and sinus infections.

Routes of application: Diffuse or apply topically on temples, wrists, throat, face or chest; blends well with basil, bergamot, black pepper, lavender, rosemary, lemon, Roman chamomile, German chamomile, *Eucalyptus globulus*, *E. radiata*, clary sage, juniper, cypress, pine, marjoram, oregano, peppermint, ravensara, thyme. Dilute four to eight drops of essential oil in 30 ml of a carrier oil for massage.

Caution: Pregnant women should consult their physician before use.

Melaleuca quinquenervia (Niaouli) *(Melaleuca quinquenervia)*

Beginnings: The Niaouli tree originated in Australia; the essential oils are steam distilled from the leaves and limbs.

Description: Fragrance is "sweet and delicate." Key constituents:

Limonene + 1,8 Cineole (55-70%)
Alpha-Pinene (7-15%)
Beta-Pinene (2-6%)
Viridiflorol (2-6%)

Therapeutic properties: This essential oil has androgen-like properties, a general tonic, anti-inflammatory, anti-infection, antibacterial, antiviral and antiparasitic (amoeba and blood parasites); relieves respiratory problems (allergies, colds, bronchitis, etc.), urinary tract problems and hemorrhoids.

Route of application: Diffuse, steam, compress, vapor rub or apply topically; basil, bergamot, black pepper, lavender, rosemary, lemon, Roman chamomile, German chamomile, *Eucalyptus globulus*, *E. radiata*, clary sage, juniper, cypress, pine, marjoram, oregano, peppermint, ravensara, thyme.

Caution: Pregnant women should consult their physician before use.

Melissa (Lemon balm) (*Melisa officinalis*)

Beginnings: The Greeks and Arabs widely used melissa in their daily lives; Paracelsus, the 16th century physician, claimed that melissa was "the elixir of life." The 17th century herbalist Gerard said that Melissa "maketh the heart merry, joyful, strengtheneth the vital spirits."

Description: Melissa is a plant native to Europe and later cultivated in the United States (Idaho and Utah); it is commonly known as "sweet balm" or "lemon balm." Melissa was the primary ingredient in Carmelite water, a combination of alcohol and essential oil distilled in France since 1611 by the Carmelite monks. Melissa is a bushy perennial of the mint family. The highly aromatic oil is distilled from the leaves, it smells like lemon. Key constituents:

Geranial (25-35%)
Neral (18-28%)
Beta Caryophyllene (12-19%)

Therapeutic properties: It has been classically used as an uplifting and calming "cure" for "melancholia"; it has tonic and anti-spasmotic properties; it is used for relieving allergies, hypertension, colds, cold sores, chicken pox, diarrhea, cholera, hypertension, dysmenorrhea, migraine and stress headaches, insomnia, insect bites, nausea and palpitations.

Routes of application: Inhalation, baths and massage. Blends well with essential oils of geranium, Roman chamomile, rose, neroli, petitgrain, frankincense, lavender, floral and citrus (typically used alone).

Mountain Savory (*Satureja Montana*)

Beginnings: The mountain savory oriinated in France. The essential oils are steam distilled from the flowering plant.

Description: Key constituents:

Carvacrol (22-35%)
Thymol (14-24%)
Gamma-Terpinene (8-15%)
Carvacrol Methyl Ether (4-9%)
Beta-Caryophyllene (3-7%)

ORAC value 113,071

Therapeutic properties: Mountain savory contains significant anti-infection properties, general tonic, relieves acute pain, relieves circulatory problems, antiseptic, stimulates healing, traditionally used to treat abscesses, burns and wounds.

Routes of application: Diffuse or apply topically mixed with a massage oil.

Caution: Pregnant women should consult their physician before use.

Myrrh (*Commiphora myrrha*)

Beginnings: The Egyptians and the Greeks viewed myrrh as a valuable commodity; it was used as their Kyphi incense to worship their gods, perform rituals, and it was commonly used in cosmetics, perfumes and herbal therapies. Myrrh was combined with frankincense for embalming purposes by the Egyptians. It is thought to be one of the substances used by the Queen of Sheba for her seduction of King Solomon. Myrrh and frankincense were given as gifts to the Christ child by the three wise men because of their antiseptic properties - remember, the Christ child was born in a stable full of animals, manure, urine, flies, bacteria and viruses. Genesis 37:25 "And they sat down to eat bread: and they lifted up their eyes and looked, and behold, a company of Ishmelites came from Gilead with their camels bearing spicery and balm and myrrh, going to carry it down to Egypt." Genesis 43:11 "And their father Israel said unto them, If it must be so now, do this; take of the best fruits in the land in your vessels, and carry down the man a present, a little balm, and a little honey, spices and myrrh, nuts, and almonds." Exodus 30:23 "Take thou also unto thee principal spices, of pure myrrh five hundred shekels, and of sweet cinnamon half so much, even two hundred and fifty shekels, and of sweet calamus two hundred and fifty shekels."

Description: A small, thorny, shrub-like tree, myrrh is native to Arabia, Somalia, Ethiopia and most North African countries. The resin is steam distilled to extract a dense, viscous yellow essential oil. The oil has a warm spicy aroma. Key constituents:

Lindestrene (30-45%)
Curzerene (17-25%)
Furanoendesma-1,3-diene (4-8%)
Methoxyfuronogermacrene (5-9%)
Beta-and Gamma-Elemenes (3-6%)

Therapeutic properties: Myrrh has anti-inflammatory and expectorant properties; it is typically used to relieve bronchitis, catarrh, coughs, colds, skin diseases, indigestion and infections of the mouth and throat.

Routes of application: Inhalation and massage. Myrrh is still used widely today in pharmaceuticals, herbal preparations and in perfumes. Myrrh blends well with frankincense, bergamot, patchouli, sandalwood, cypress, juniper, geranium, lavender, lemon, palmarosa, tea tree, *Eucalyptus radiata*, rosemary, Roman chamomile, grapefruit, pine, vetiver, ylang-ylang, all spice oils, camphor and lavender.

Caution: Pregnant women should consult their physician before use.

Myrtle (*Myrtus communis*)

Beginnings: The myrtle tree originated in Tunisia and Morocco. Nehemiah 8:15 "And that they should publish and proclaim in all their cities, and in Jerusalem, saying, Go forth unto the mount, and fetch olive branches, and pine branches, and myrtle branches, and palm branches, and branches of thick trees, to make booths, as it is written."

Isaiah 41:19 "I will plant in the wilderness the cedar, the shittah tree, and the myrtle, and the oil tree; I will set in the desert the fir tree, and the pine, and the box tree together." Isaiah 55:13 "Instead of the thorn shall come up the fir tree, and instead of the brier shall come up the myrtle tree: and it shall be to the Lord for a name, for an everlasting sign that shall not be cut off."

Description: The essential oils of myrtle are steam distilled from the leaves. Key constituents:

Alpha Pinene (45-60%)
1,8 Cineol (Eucalyptol) (17-27%)
Limonene (5-11%)
Linalol (2-5%)

Therapeutic properties: Expectorant, anti-infectious, liver stimulant, prostate decongestant, mild antispasmodic, tonic for the skin (acne, blemishes, oily skin, psoriasis, etc.), thyroid and ovaries. Relieves bronchitis, coughs, decongestant, hypothyroidism, insomnia, sinus infections, asthma, cystitis, diarrhea, dysentery, indigestion, hemorrhoids; particularly useful for children with respiratory complaints and coughs.

Routes of application: Diffuse, humidifier, topical. Blends well with bergamot, lavender, lemon, lemongrass, *Melaleuca alternifolia*, rosewood, rosemary, spearmint and thyme.

Neroli (bitter orange) (*Citrus aurantium*)

Beginnings: The use of neroli was first recorded by the Egyptians and Romans. In 1680, neroli was named after the Prince of Nerola, Flavio Orsini from Italy. He went to great effort to ensure a steady supply of the essential oil to scent the bath water and the gloves of his wife Anna-Maria de la Tremoille Orsini, Princess of Nerola - she brought the neroli fragrance into fashion with the Italian aristocracy.

Description: Neroli is commonly known as orange blossom; it is produced from the white blossoms of the bitter orange tree which was first discovered in China. Bitter orange is cultivated in orchards in Egypt, Morocco, Algeria, the United States, Italy and southern France. The pale yellow oil is expensive to produce - it takes one ton of blossoms to produce two pounds of oil. The oil is distilled from the blossoms still in the bud stage. Key constituents:

Linalol (28-44%)
Limonene (9-18%)
Beta-Pinene (7-17%)
Linalyl Acetate (3-15%)
Trans-Ocimene (3-8%)
Alpha Terpineol (2.5-5%)
Trans-Nerolidol (1-5%)
Myrcene (1-4%)

Therapeutic properties: Used commonly as a sedative and anti-depressant; neroli is used to relieve anxiety, hysteria, insomnia, dysmenorrhea, PMS, shock, palpitations, circulatory problems, skin problems, hemorrhoids, anti-infectious, antibacterial, antiparasitic, relieves hypertension, digestive problems and menopausal symptoms.

Routes of application: Inhalation, baths, topical and massage. Blends well with cedarwood, coriander, frankincense, mandarin, geranium, ginger, jasmine, lavender, lemon, orange, rose, ylang-ylang, yuzu and sandalwood.

Nutmeg (*Myristica fragrans*)

Beginnings: Nutmeg originated in Tunisia and Indonesia. This spicy essential oil was traditionally used to increase muscle and joint circulation.

Description: The essential oil of nutmeg is steam distilled from the fruit and seeds. Key constituents:

Sabinene (14-29%)
Beta-Pinene (13-18%)
Alpha-Pinene (15-28%)
Limonene (2-7%)

Gamma-Terpinene (2-6%)
Terpinene-4-ol (2-6%)
Myristicine (5-12%)

Therapeutic Properties: The essential oil of nutmeg is antiseptic, antiparasitic, analgesic, relieves PMS and dysmenorrhea, rheumatism, circulatory and nervous system tonic, relieves fatigue and supports the immune system; it improves appetite and digestion. The essential oil of nutmeg has adrenal cortex-like properties, relieves frigidity, impotence, gout, nausea and peripheral neuropathies.

Routes of application: Apply topically diluted with extender oil. Nutmeg blends well with cinnamon, clove, cypress, frankincense, lemon, *Melaleuca alternifolia*, Melissa, orange, patchouli, rosemary oils.

Caution: Pregnant women should consult their physician before use; individuals with seizure disorders should avoid the use of nutmeg oil.

Orange (*Citrus sinensis, C. aurantium*)

Beginnings: China was the birth place of the orange tree. The orange tree was transplanted to the Mediterranean from China and Asia by the Saracens during the Crusades; it is now grown in Sicily, Israel, Spain and the United States - the essential oil has different medicinal characteristics depending on the country of origin. The fragrant oil was used for culinary, cosmetic and medicinal purposes.

Description: The sweet and bitter oils are extracted mechanically by pressing the fresh orange peel. The oil ranges from yellow to brown in color and will ignite at a low temperature of 75 F. Key constituents:

Limonene (85-96%)
Myrcene (0.5-3%)

ORAC value 18,898

Therapeutic properties: Orange oil is used as a tonic for anxiety and depression, relieves jaundice, scurvy, heartburn, angina, palpitations, cardiac spasm, lowers cholesterol, mouth ulcers, edema, insomnia, chronic bronchitis, respiratory infections, colds, prolapse of the uterus and the anus, hemorrhoids, indigestion and constipation and oral ulcers. The essential oil is rich in vitamin C.

Routes of application: Baths and massage. Orange oil is used widely in the packaged food (chocolate-orange candies) and cosmetic industries. Blends well with bay, bergamot, black pepper, cinnamon, clove, coriander, cypress, frankincense, geranium, grapefruit, jasmine, juniper, lavender, lemon, *Litsea cubeba*, marjoram, neroli, nutmeg, patchouli, petitgrain, sandalwood, rosewood, vetiver and ylang-ylang. oils.

Cautions: Pregnant women should consult their physician before use; the user of orange oil topically should avoid direct sunlight or UV light for at least 72 hours; limit bath applications to four drops per bath as excess orange oil can irritate sensitive skin.

Oregano (*Origanum compactum*)

Beginnings: Oregano originated in Utah, Turkey and France.

Description: A densely branched perennial herb growing to 20 inches. Oregano essential oils are steam distilled from the oval leaves and pink flowers of the plant. Key Constituents:

Carvacrol (60-75%)
Gamma-Terpinene (3.5-8.5%)
Para-Cymene (5.5-9%)
Beta Caryophyllene (2-5%)
Myrcene (1-3%)
Thymol (0-5%)

ORAC value 153,007

Therapeutic properties: Potent anti-infectious essential oil for respiratory infections, gastroenteritis, genital infections, nerve tonic, blood and lymphatic tonic; it has a broad spectrum antiseptic property against bacteria, mycobacteria (tuberculosis), fungus, yeast, viruses and parasites; it is a general tonic and will stimulate the immune system; relieves asthma, bronchitis, pulmonary tuberculosis, rheumatism and whooping cough, digestive problems and pneumonia.

Routes of application: Oil of oregano can be applied topically to the bottom of the feet without dilution; dilute with extender oil when applied to other parts of the body. Oregano oil blends well with essential oils of bay, basil, bergamot, cypress, eucalyptus, fennel, geranium, lemon, lemongrass, *Litsea cubeba*, myrtle, orange, petitegrain, pine, Roman chamomile, rosemary and thyme.

Caution: high phenol content can irritate the skin, therefore dilute with extender oils at the rate of one drop oregano oil to 50 drops of a massage oil; avoid contact with all mucus membranes; pregnant women should consult physician before use. It is a good idea to test skin for sensitivity.

Palmarosa (*Cymbopogon martini*)

Beginnings: Palmarosa grass originated in India and Conoros. Historically was called "Turkish geranium oil" or "East Indian geranium oil." Because the high geranil content produces a rose-like odor, palmarosa is often used to adulterate rose essential oil.

Description: Palmarosa is related to lemongrass; the oil is steam distilled from the leaves. Key constituents:

Geraniol (70-85%)
Geranyl Acetate (6-10%)
Linalol (3-7%)

Therapeutic properties: Antimicrobial, antibacterial, antifungal, antiviral, cardiotonic and uterine tonic; used to relieve yeast infections including candida, beneficial for the cardiovascular system, circulation, digestion, infection, nervous system, skin conditions, athlete's foot and rashes.

Routes of application: Apply topically; palmarosa oil blends well with basil, fennel, geranium, lemongrass, myrtle, pine, rosemary and thyme.

Caution: Pregnant women should consult their physician before use.

Parsley (*Petroselinum sativum*)

Beginnings: There was a medieval belief that parsley could only be grown in the gardens of honest men and women. Parsley was chewed to "repel the devil."

Description: Parsley was a native plant of Asia Minor, it is now cultivated commercially and in home gardens around the world. The oil is extracted by distillation from the ripe parsley seeds and leaves. Parsley is used for culinary and herbal medicinal purposes. Key constituents:

p-mentha-1,3,8-triene (6-60%)
Myristicin (7-33%)
Parsley Apiol (trace-18%)
Elemicin (0.2-3%)

Therapeutic properties: Parsley is used as a diuretic, kidney diseases, urinary infections and relieving edema. Parsley is considered to contain high levels of vitamin A and iron and is used to promote healthy hair, skin, teeth, eyes, relieve anemia, support liver function, "clears" toxins, calms the nervous system and relieves symptoms of dysmenorrhea and menopause.

Routes of application: Massage is a common way to deliver the essential oil. Parsley oil blends well with fennel, lemon and rosemary oils.

Patchouli (*Pogostemon patchouli, P. cablin*)

Beginnings: Alongside of rose, jasmine, sandalwood and basil, patchouli was a favorite essential oil used in India; shawls and blankets were impregnated with the oil. It was historically used as an aphrodisiac and was reintroduced as an aphrodisiac in herbal preparations in the 1960s. The word patchouli comes from the south Indian Tamil language, patch, meaning "green" and ilai meaning "leaf."

Description: The essential oil is extracted by steam distillation from the dried and fermented leaves of the small, hairy perennial shrub. The oil is characterized by an intense, woody, sweet-spicy balsamic aroma. The oil gains in quality over time. Key constituents:

Patchoulol (25-35%)
Alpha-Bulnesene (14-20%)
Alpha-Guaiene + Seychellene (15-25%)
Alpha-Patchoulene (5-9%)

Therapeutic properties: Patchouli has significant astringent and diuretic properties and is used to enhance scalp and skin health, relieves wrinkles, dandruff, acne, eczema, hemorrhoids and reduces scars. The oil is a general tonic and is traditionally used to relieve anxiety and depression.

Routes of application: Inhalation, massage and baths. Small quantities have a stimulating effect while larger doses have a sedative effect. Blends well with bergamot, clary sage, frankincense, geranium, ginger, lavender, lemongrass, myrrh, pine, rosewood and sandalwood.

Peppermint (*Mentha piperata*)

Beginnings: The Egyptians originally used peppermint to flavor wine and food and it was historically said to be an aphrodisiac. According to Greek mythology the genus Mentha takes its name from the nymph Minthe, who was seduced by Pluto and turned into a plant by his jealous wife, who stomped Minthe into the ground. Pluto turned her into the herb, knowing that Minthe would then be appreciated by many people for thousands of years. Culpepper, the 17th century herbalist, stated that peppermint was "the herb most useful for complaints of the stomach, such as wind and vomiting, for which there are few remedies of greater efficiency."

Description: The leaves of the peppermint plant are shorter and broader than spearmint and are characterized by large spikes of purple flowers. Peppermint is a British classic herb that was spread around the world during their colonial reign. The colorless peppermint oil is distilled from the partially dried leaves and stems. It is commonly used in beverages, ice cream, sauces and jellies, liqueurs, medicines, toothpastes and mouth washes, cleaners, cosmetics, tobacco, desserts and chewing gums. Key constituents:

Menthol (34-44%)
Menthone (12-20%)
Menthofurane (4-9%)
1,8 Cineol (Euclyptol) (2-5%)
Pulegone (2-5%)
Menthyl Acetate (4-10%)

Therapeutic properties: Peppermint and peppermint oil is used to relieve indigestion, heart burn, varicose veins, hemorrhoids, hot flashes, dysmenorrhea, congestion, skin disorders, itching of ringworm, herpes blisters, scabies, poison oak and poison ivy, muscle spasm, arthritis, rheumatism, colds, throat infections, flu, flatulence, headaches, nausea, toothache and sunburn.

Routes of application: Inhalation, tea, baths and massage. It blends well with basil, pine, lemon, geranium, rosemary, tea tree, lavender, eucalyptus, grapefruit, juniper, cypress, black pepper, niaouli and ravensara.

Cautions: For skin complaints, use peppermint oil in concentrations of less than one percent as higher doses can cause skin irritation; pregnant women should use mint tea for nausea instead of the purified essential oil.

Petitgrain (*Citrus aurantium, C. amara, C. brigaradier*)

Beginnings: The petitgrain comes from the word for little fruit or little grains. In 1694 the essential oil was distilled from the small unripe fruit called orangettes, which are seeds or kernels.

Description: The essential oil is steam distilled from the tips of the fresh leaves, small twigs and in very high quality oil the small unripe green fruit is used. Key constituents:

Linalyl Acetate
Linalol
Geranyl Acetate
Nerol
Terpineol
Nerolidol

Therapeutic properties: The essential oil is antispasmodic, antidepressant, stimulant, tonic, calmative, anti-infectious, antiseptic and has nervine properties; it is used in the treatment of nervous conditions, acne, insomnia, depression, general debility, anxiety, stress-related conditions, indigestion and skin disorders.

Routes of application: The essential oil of petitgrain blends well with rosemary, clove, cedarwood, cypress, *Eucalyptus citriodora*, frankincense, geranium, jasmine, juniper, lavender, lemon, mandarin, marjoram, neroli, orange, palmarosa, patchouli, rose maroc, rose otto, sandalwood, ylang ylang and yuzu.

Pine (*Pinus sylvestris, P. palustris, P. abies*)

Beginnings: The pine, also known as the "Scottish pine." This tree is cultivated for wood, cellulose, tar, pitch, turpentine and essential oils. The Scandinavians had traditionally used pine oils in their saunas and steam baths for their refreshing and antiseptic qualities.
An ancient Egyptian cookbook describes the use of "pine nuts" as a highly nutritious food.

Description: The pine grows wild and is cultivated throughout Europe, North America and the former USSR. Pine oil comes from the heartwood of the tree, however, the finest quality of pine oil is distilled from the pine needles. The clear thick oil is characterized by a fresh aroma with a resinous woody undertone. Key constituents:

Alpha Pinene (55-70%)
Beta Pinene (3-8%)
Limonene (5-10%)
Delta 3 Carene (6-12%)
Sylvestrene
Pumilone
Dipentene
Cadinene

Therapeutic properties: Acts as an antiseptic and adrenal tonic; pine oils are especially useful for the relief of respiratory complaints including bronchitis, catarrh, colds, coughs and sinusitis; cystitis and urinary infections; and arthritis, fibromyalgia and aches and pains.

Routes of application: Inhalation, baths and massage. Pine oil is commonly used in balms, body rubs, soaps, bath oils and as a shoe deodorizer and disinfectant. The essential oil of pine blends well with bergamot, cedarwood, clary sage, cypress, *Eucalyptus radiata*, frankincense, grapefruit, juniper, lavender, lemon, marjoram, *Melaleuca alternifolia*, peppermint, ravensara, rosemary, sandalwood and thyme.

Ravensara (*Ravensara aromatica*)

Beginnings: The ravensara plant originated in Madagascar; the essential oils are referred to by the people of Madagascar as "the oil that heals." The bark of the tree is used as an ingredient in the production of a local rum; the seeds are known as Madagascan nutmeg and are used in cooking and folk medicine.

Description: The tree is characterized by a pungent aromatic dark, smooth evergreen leaves. It produces flowers and seeds which are used as cooking spices. The essential oil is steam distilled from the leaves and branches. Key constituents:

Limonene + Eucalyptol (50-65%)
Sabinene (6-12%)
Alpha-Terpineol (5-11%)
Alpha-Pinene (4-9%)
Beta-Pinene (1-5%)

Monoterpenes- Alpha and Beta-pinene; Sesquiterpenes; Monoterpenols; Terpene esters; terpenyle acetate; Terpene oxides; 1,8 cineole.

Therapeutic properties: The oils of ravensara are anti-infectious, antiviral, antibacterial, expectorant, antimicrobial; it acts as a tonic for the nervous and respiratory system; relieves bronchitis, asthma, cystitis, burns, cholera, herpes, infectious mononucleosis, insomnia, muscle fatigue, rhinopharyngitis, shingles, sinusitis and viral hepatitis; disinfects and stimulates healing of cuts, scrapes and wounds.

Routes of application: Diffuse or apply topically. Ravensara blends well with bay, bergamot, black pepper, cardamom, cedarwood, clary sage, cypress, eucalyptus, geranium, frankincense, ginger, grapefruit, lavender, mandarin, marjoram, lemon, palmarosa, pine, rosemary, sandalwood, tea tree and thyme.

Caution: Pregnant women should consult their physician before use.

Rose (Maroc/*Rosa centifolia,* Otto/ *R. damascena*)

Beginnings: The word rose comes from the Greek "roden" which translates to red - the original rose is thought to have been crimson. In ancient myth, the rose sprang from the blood of Adonis or Venus. The rose and rose oils have been revered before the beginnings of the Roman Empire; the rose was used in garlands, scented bathes, perfumes and for ostentatious public events. Rosebushes were brought to Bulgaria by Turkish merchants; traditionally, the rose bush was grown as a dense hedge as a living fence around wheat and bean fields, between rows of trees and home gardens. The first recorded commercial distillery was started in 1612 in Shiraz, Persia (Iran).

Description: The Damascena rose is cultivated in Bulgaria, where the flowers are picked at dawn and the yellow-brown oil is extracted by enfleurage within 24 hours. It takes five tons of rose flowers to produce two pounds of rose oil. The Centifolia rose is cultivated in France, Algeria, Morocco and Egypt. The essential oil from the rose is the least toxic of all of the oils. Key constituents:

Geraniol (12-28%)
Citronellol (34-44%)
Farnesol
Methyl Eugenol
Nerol (6-9%)
Phenylethylic Alcohol (0-2%)

Therapeutic properties: Rose oil is revered as an aphrodisiac, mood enhancer, general tonic, relieves circulatory problems, constipation, headaches, mental fatigue, skin disorders, dysmenorrheal and menopausal problems. The Bulgarian *Rosa damascene* (high in citronellol) is significantly different from the Moroccan *Rosa centifolia* (high in phenyl ethanol) - they are characterized by different colors, aromas and therapeutic properties.

Routes of application: Baths, inhalation and massage. Rose essential oil blends well with jasmine, neroli, geranium, lavender, clary sage, sandalwood, lemon, Roman chamomile, mandarin, ylang-ylang, petitgrain, vetiver, bergamot and patchouli.

Caution: Pregnant women should consult with their physician before use.

Rosemary (*Rosmarinus officinalis*)

Beginnings: The Egyptians were the first culture to actively use rosemary. The popularity of rosemary soon moved into 1000 B.C. Greece and Rome who used the essential oils to symbolize love and death. During outbreaks of the plague, rosemary was burned in public places and worn as garlands around the neck as an antiseptic. Rosemary was an original ingredient of the "Marseilles Vinegar" a.k.a. "Four Thieves Vinegar" used by grave robbers and bandits to protect themselves during the 15th century plague. The name of the plant is derived from the Latin words for "dew of the sea" (ros + marinus). All ancient healers used rosemary, including the 16th century Swiss physician and alchemist, Paracelsus.

Description: Rosemary is a small shrub that grows to three foot in height; it is characterized by grey-green needle-like leaves, pale blue-white flowers. The clear oil is steam-distilled from the flowers and leaves and has a "warm woody aroma." Key constituents:

1,8 Cineol (Eucalyptol) (38-55%)
Alpha-Pinene (9-14%)
Beta-Pinene (4-9%)
Camphor (5-15%)
Camphene (2.5-6%)
Borneol (1.5-5%)
Limonene (1-4%)

ORAC value 3,309

Therapeutic properties: Rosemary oil is revered as a stimulant for the circulation, memory; it can relieve rheumatism, myalgia, hepatitis, PMS, hypertension, alopecia, colds, cold sores, canker sores, bronchitis, burns, dandruff, indigestion, diarrhea, flatulence, asthma and headaches.

Routes of application: Baths and massage. Rosemary oil can be inhaled from a handkerchief for headaches and to clear sinuses. The oil of rosemary blends well with the oils of basil, bergamot, black pepper, cedarwood, cypress, *Eucalyptus radiata*, frankincense, geranium, juniper, lavender, lemon, *Litsea cubeba*, mandarin, marjoram, naiouli, oregano, peppermint, pine and ravensara oils.

Cautions: Use in low concentrations as high doses have reportedly caused seizures. Do not use in the first trimester of pregnancy or in individuals who have high blood pressure.

Rosewood (*Aniba rosaeodora*)

Beginnings: The rosewood tree originates from Brazil; the essential oil is steam distilled from the wood.

Description: Key constituents:

Linalol (70-90%)
Alpha-Terpineol (2-7%)
Alpha-Copaene (Trace-3%)
1,8 Cineole (Eucalyptol) (Trace-3%)
Geraniol (0.5-2.5%)

Therapeutic properties: Anti-infectious, antibacterial, antiviral, antiparasitic, antifungal; relieves acne, candida, depression, eczema, oral infections, skin problems and vaginitis.

Routes of application: Diffuse or apply topically.

Cautions: Pregnant women should consult their physician before use.

Sage (*Salvia officinalis, S. sclarea* - Clary sage)

Beginnings: Sage is considered to be a sacred herb by many cultures; it was used to enhance female fertility; and the Chinese have used sage as a medicinal herb for thousands of years.

Description: There are many varieties of common sage, they are all shrubby herbs characterized by rough wrinkled leaves. The essential oil is distilled from the leaves and has a potent, fresh and spicy aroma with a mild camphor overtone. Key constituents:

Alpha-Thuyone (18-4350
Beta-Thuyone (3-8.5%)
1,8 Cineole (Eucalyptol) (5.5-13%)
Camphor (4.5-24.5%)
Camphene (1.5-7%)
Alpha-Pinene (1-6.5%)
Alpha-Humulene (0-12%)

Monoterpenes: Alpha-thujene, Alpha-pinene, camphene, myrcene, limonene; Sesquiterpenes; Hydrocarbons; Esters; Phenols: thymol; Oxides (15%): 1,8 cineole; Monoterpenones (20-70%): alpha thujone (12-33%), beta-thujone (2-14%), camphor (1-26%); Aldehydes; Coumarins.

Therapeutic properties: Sage oil is a general tonic; it is used to relieve dysmenorrhea, arthritis, aches, infections, sore throat and edema. Clary sage is used for its sedative and euphoric effects; it is used to relieve insomnia, anxiety and depression. Its aroma is more floral than that of the common sage.

Routes of application: Bath and massage. Sage oil blends well with bergamot, lavender, lemon, peppermint, lemongrass, pine and rosemary.

Cautions: In high doses sage can produce significant stimulation and should be avoided by those with seizure disorders. All varieties of sage should be avoided during the first trimester of pregnancy.

Sandalwood (*Santalum album*)

Beginnings: Sandalwood was first used by the Chinese, Indians and Egyptians 4,000 years ago. It was used for perfumes for more than 2,000 years, cosmetics and furniture. Religious pilgrims used sandalwood to cover themselves during worship.

Description: The sandalwood tree is an evergreen that grows to thirty feet in height. It is cultivated in Indonesia, Southeast Asia and in eastern India. The young sandalwood tree grows as a parasite on other trees for the first seven years after germination, the oil is not distilled from the roots and the heartwood until the tree is at least 30 years old. The syrupy, balsamic oil is extracted from coarsely chipped and powdered heartwood and root wood by steam distillation. Key constituents:

Alpha-Santalol (47-55%)
Beta-Santalol (19-23%)
Sesquiterpinol Santalol
Santenonol
Teresantalal
Borneol
Santalene

Therapeutic properties: Sandalwood is used to relieve depression and tension; it is an expectorant, aphrodisiac and anti-spasmodic and is commonly used to relieve bronchitis, coughs, nausea, cystitis and skin conditions.

Routes of application: Inhalation and massage. Sandalwood oil blends well with black pepper, clary sage, clove, palmarosa, petitgrain, cypress, frankincense, lemon, myrrh, orange, patchouli, Roman chamomile, spruce, ylang-ylang, neroli and rose oils.

Spearmint (*Mentha spicata*)

Beginnings: The spearmint plant originated in Utah. Spearmint oil is steam distilled from the leaves.

Description: Key constituents:

Carvone (45-55%)
Cis-Dihydrocarvone (5-10%)
Limonene (15-25%)

ORAC value 5,398

Therapeutic properties: Relieves bronchitis, candida, cystitis and hypertension; it is an anti-inflammatory, calming agent, astringent, antiseptic, mucolytic, stimulates gallbladder and relieves dysmenorrhea. Spearmint oil is a tonic for the respiratory and nervous systems; it stimulates appetite and can help relieve halitosis, depression, indigestion, dry skin, eczema, headaches, nausea, sore gums, vaginitis and obesity.

Routes of application: Diffuse or apply topically. Spearmint oil blends well with basil, lavender, peppermint and rosemary.

Caution: Pregnant women should consult their physician before use.

Spikenard (*Nardostachys jatamansi*)

Beginnings: Spikenard originated in India and was historically used as a perfume, and as a medicinal oil. The oil is extracted from the roots by steam distillation. Song of Solomon 1:12 "While the king sitteth at his table, my spikenard sendeth forth the smell thereof" Song of Solomon 4:13 "Thy plants an orchard of pomegranates, with pleasant fruits; camphire with spikenard." Song of Solomon 4:14 "Spikenard and saffron; calamus and cinnamon, with all trees of frankincense; myrrh and aloes, with all the chief spices." John 12 "Then took Mary a pound of ointment of spikenard, very costly, and anointed the feet of Jesus."

Description: Spikenard is a perennial herb that produces a straight stem, green leaves, and small pinkish-mauve bell-shaped flowers. The essential oil is steam distilled from the plant roots. Key constituents:

Calarene (22-35%)
Beta-Ionene (4-8%)
Beta-Maaliene (4-9%)
Aristoladiene (3-7%)
Valeranone
Jonon
Tetramethyloxatricycloclecanol
Methylthymyl-Ether
1,8-Cineole

Therapeutic properties: The oil is antibacterial, antifungal, anti-inflammatory, deodorant, relaxing and a skin tonic; it relieves allergies, candida, indigestion, insomnia, dysmenorrhea, migraine, nausea, rashes, bacterial infections, stress, rapid heart rate (tachycardia) and tension.

Routes of application: Apply to the abdomen or topically to affected area. Blends well with lavender, lemon, clary sage, clove, juniper, cypress, geranium, rose maroc, neroli, frankincense, myrrh, patchouli, pine and vetiver.

Caution: If pregnant consult physician before use.

Spruce (*Picea mariana*)

Beginning: The spruce originated in Canada; the essential oil is steam distilled from the needles and twigs. The Lakota Native Americans used spruce to facilitate prayers to the Great Spirit.

Description: Key constituents:
- Bornyl Acetate (18-28%)
- Camphene (17-25%)
- Alpha Pinene (12-19%)
- Beta Pinene (4-8%)
- Delta-3-Carene (5-10%)
- Limonene (2-7%)
- Santene (1-5%)
- Tricyclene (1-5%)

Therapeutic properties: Spruce oil is used to relieve arthritis, rheumatism, bone pain; it acts as a general glandular tonic, relieves candida, hyperthyroidism and prostatitis.

Routes of application: Diffuse or apply topically. Spruce essential oil blends well with wintergreen, birch, *Eucalyptus radiata,* frankincense, helichrysum and ravensara.

Caution: Pregnant women should consult their physician before use.

Tagetes (*Tagetes glanulifera*)

Beginnings: Historically used as an insecticide. It was hung in doorways, stuffed in mattresses and worn as garlands to repel mosquitoes, flies and ticks. The essential oil has been used to kill maggots in open wounds.

Description: Tagetes is a weed that grows up to six feet tall; it has deep green divided leaves and large numbers of yellow-orange flowers that resemble daisy heads. The essential oil is steam distilled from the leaves, stalks and flowers, preferably harvested when the seeds are just beginning to develop. Key constituents:

- Ocimenes
- Dihydro Tageton
- Dihydrotagetone
- Thymol

Therapeutic properties: The essential oil of tagetes has anti-infectious, antifungal, antibiotic, antispasmodic, emmenagogue, mucolytic, antiparasitic and antiseptic properties; it is used to treat athlete's foot, corns, calluses, bunions, catarrh, coughs, chest infections, parasitic infestations and fungal infestations.

Routes of application: The essential oil of tagetes blends well with bergamot, clary sage, lemon and lavender.

Cautions: Pregnant women should consult their doctor before using this oil; not to be used in children under the age of 16 years; it may cause skin irritation on sensitive skin; may cause photosensitivity.

Tansy (Blue) (*Tanacetum annuum*)

Beginnings: The tansy plant originated in Morocco and France; the essential oil is steam distilled from the leaves and flowers.

Description: Key Constituents:

Camphor (10-17%)
Sabinene (10-17%)
Beta-Pinene (5-10%)
Myrcene (7-13%)
Alpha-Phellandrene (5-10%)
Para-Cymene (3-8%)
Chamazulene (3-6%)

Therapeutic properties: Blue tansy Isanti-inflammatory, relieves pain, relieves pruritits, sedates the nervous system, has antihistamine, hypotensive and hormone-like activities.

Routes of application: Topical and diffuse.

Cautions: Pregnant women should consult their physician before use.

Tarragon (*Artemisia dracunculus*)

Beginnings: The tarragon plant originates in Slovenia and France. Tarragon was traditionally used in Europe as an antimicrobial and antiseptic. The essential oil is steam distilled from the leaves.

Description: Key constituents:

Methyl Chavicol (Estragole) (68-80%)
Trans-Beta Ocimene (6-12%)
Cis-Beta-Ocimene (6-12%)
Limonene (2-6%)

Therapeutic properties: Relieves colitis, hiccups, intestinal spasm, parasites, rheumatic pain and sciatica; used for genital and urinary tract infections, nausea, PMS, dysmenorrhea, nerve tonic and wound healing.

Routes of application: Topically diluted with carrier oil; blends well with chamomile, clary sage, fir, juniper, lavender, pine, rosewood, orange and tangerine oils.

Cautions: Pregnant women should consult physician before use.

Tea Tree (*Melaleuca alternifolia*) See Melaleuca.

Beginnings: The antiseptic properties of tea tree oil were appreciated by the Australian Aborigines centuries ago; they used tea tree oil medicinally for treating sunburn, ringworm and athletes foot; tea tree oil was used to treat snake bite. In World War II, cutters and producers of tea tree oil were exempt from military service until a plentiful supply of tea tree oil was stocked; the essential oil was issued to each soldier and sailor for them to treat tropical infections and wounds.

Description: The tea tree, also known as the swamp tree and the "paper bark" tree, is a native plant of Australia and Tasmania; it produces white hanging flowers on a long spike. The pale green essential oil is extracted from the twigs and leaves and has a strong aromatic camphorous odor similar to eucalyptus. Key constituents:

Gamma Terpinene (10-28%)
Alpha-Terpinene (5-13%)
1,8 Cineole (Eucalyptol) (0-15%)
Alpha-Terpineol (1.5-8%)
Para-Cymene (0.5-12%)
Terpineol -4 (30-45%)
Limonene (0.5-4%)
Aromadendrene (trace-7%)
Delta-Cadinene (trace-8%)
Alpha Pinene (1-6%)

Therapeutic properties: Tea tree oil is a potent all-purpose disinfectant and antiseptic and is commonly used to relieve flea infestations, respiratory problems, bronchitis, laryngitis, skin conditions, athlete's foot, burns, cold sores, mouth ulcers, verrucas, thrush and warts.

Routes of application: Inhalation, topical, mouth wash and baths. Tea tree oil blends well with basil, bergamot, black pepper, lavender, rosemary, lemon, Roman chamomile, German chamomile, *Eucalyptus globulus*, *Eucalyptus radiata*, clary sage, juniper, cypress, pine, marjoram, oregano, peppermint, ravensera and thyme.

Cautions: Oxidized tea tree oil smells like melted rubber.

Thyme *(Thymus vulgaris)*

Beginnings: The ancient Egyptian embalmers mixed thyme oil in their embalming fluids. The Greeks drank an herbal infusion of thyme leaves after large banquets to aid digestion. Nicholas Culpeper claimed that thyme was "a great lung strengthener and a remedy for shortness of breath." Rudyard Kipling wrote, ""'wind-bit thyme that smells like the perfume of the dawn in paradise."

Description: Thyme is a low-growing wild herb characterized by dark green leaves, woody stalks and small pink flowers. Thyme is cultivated widely throughout the Mediterranean, Algeria, Yugoslavia and Egypt for culinary and pharmaceutical uses. The essential oil is extracted from the whole plant by steam-distillation and has a pungent, sweet herbaceous aroma. The first steam distillation produces a red essential oil, the second distillation produces a clear oil. Key constituents:

Thymol (37-55%)
Para-Cymene (14-28%)
Gamma-Terpinene (4-11%)
Linalol (3-6.5%)
Carvacrol (0.5-5.5%)
Myrcine (1-2.8%)

ORAC value 159,590

Therapeutic properties: Thyme is used to relieve fatigue and anxiety, rheumatic aches, asthma, pertussis, laryngitis, tonsillitis, bronchitis, colitis, cystitis, dermatitis, psoriasis, sciatica, and vaginal yeast infections; relieves insomnia, depression, indigestion, headaches, obesity, skin conditions and as an antiseptic to treat viral infections, coughs and a wide variety of respiratory infections.

Routes of application: Inhalation, compresses, salves, baths and massage; blends well with bergamot, citrus oils, cedarwood, cypress, eucalyptus, geranium, juniper, *Melaleuca alternifolia*, oregano, pine, rosemary, grapefruit, clary sage, lemon,
and tea tree oils.

Cautions: Pregnant women should consult with their physician before use; undiluted thyme essential oil can irritate the skin.

Tsuga (*Tsuga Canadensis*)

Beginnings: This plant originated in Canada; the essential oil is steam distilled from the needles and twigs of a conifer evergreen tree commercially marketed as "hemlock."

Description: Key constituents:

Alpha-and Beta-Pinenes (18-25%)
Camphene (12-18%)
Limonene + Beta Phellandrene (3-7%)
Bornyl Acetate (28-38%)
Tricyclene (4-8%)
Myrcene (1-3%)

Therapeutic properties: The essential oil is analgesic, antirheumatic, astringent, tonic; relieves coughs, respiratory problems, kidney problems, skin problems, urinary tract infections and venereal infections.

Routes of application: Diffuse, massage and apply topically; dilute one drop of oil with one teaspoon of carrier oil.

Cautions: Pregnant women should consult with their physician before use; repeated use in a short period of time can produce sensitivity.

Valerian (*Valeriana officinalis*)

Beginnings: This herb originated in Belgium, Croatia and France; the essential oil is steam distilled from the root.

Description: The tall thin stalk produces a small round flower head of tiny, white-pink flowers. An essential oil that smells more "woodsy" is produced from the Japanese "kesso root" and from the Indian valerian (*V. wallichi*). Key constituents:

Bornyl Acetate (32-44%)
Camphene + Alpha-Fenchene (24-34%)
Alpha-Pinene (4-8%)
Beta-Pinene (2-6%)
Isobicycolgermacrenol (3-6%)
Myrtenyl Acetate (1-5%)

Therapeutic properties: Relieves insomnia, nervous indigestion, migraine, restlessness, stress, hypothermia and tension; it has sedative and tranquilizing properties.

Routes of application: Diffuse, inhale, massage or apply topically; blends well with cedarwood, lavender, mandarin, patchouli, petitgrain, pine and rosemary.

Cautions: Pregnant women should consult their physician before use.

Vetiver (vetivert) (*Vetiveria zizanioides*)

Beginnings: Originated in Haiti and India; it is steam distilled from the root. In India the roots are woven into fans and screens called "tatties" for doors, windows and floors to give rooms a good fragrance and repel insects.

Description: Vetiver grows as a clump of thin grass-like leaves. The roots are spindly but intensely aromatic; many claim the essential oil smells like "dirt." Key constituents:

Alpha Vetivone (3-6%)
Beta Vetivone (3-6%)
Khusenol (6-11%)
Isovalencenol (11-15%)
Nootkatone (2-5%)
Khusimone (3-6%)

Therapeutic properties: Vetiver oil is antiseptic, antispasmodic, calming, rubifacient, sedative, stimulant and tonic for the circulatory system and bone marrow; relieves acne, anxiety, arthritis pain, cuts, depression, insomnia and oily skin.

Route of application: Diffuse, massage or apply topically; blends well with bergamot, black pepper, clary sage, *Eucalyptus citriodora*, geranium, ginger, grapefruit, jasmine, lavender, lemon, lemongrss, litsea cubeba, mandarin, melissa, orange, patchouli, rose, sandalwood, ylang-ylang and yuzu oils.

Cautions: Pregnant women should consult their physician before use.

Vitex (chaste tree) (*Vitex negundo*)

Beginnings: This tree originated in Turkey; the essential oil is steam distilled from the inner bark, small branches and leaves of the chaste tree.

Description: Key constituents:

Beta-Caryophyllene (38-48%)
Limonene + 1,8 Cineole (3-7%)
Sabinene (10-15%)
Caryophyllene Oxide (5-10%)
Longifolene + Alpha-Gurjunene (5-10%)

Therapeutic properties: Relieves symptoms of Parkinson's disease and neurological disease.

Routes of application: Diffuse or apply topically diluted with base oils; rub two to three drops in palms, cup over nose and inhale; mix two to four drops with one teaspoon of salt and add to warm bath water.

Cautions: pregnant women should consult their physician before use.

Wintergreen (*Gaultheria procumbens*)

Beginnings: The tree originated in China; the essential oil is steam distilled from the leaves. Wintergreen leaves and bark were used to replace tea as a drink during the American Civil War.

Description: Key constituents:
Methyl Salicylate (90+%)

Therapeutic properties: The essential oil is antispasmodic, anti-inflammatory and a liver tonic. Wintergreen essential oils have been used to relieve arthritis, rheumatism, inflammation, fibromyalgia, pain of tendonitis, high blood pressure and muscle spasms and cramps; Wintergreen essential oil has been used to relieve cystitis, urinary bladder infections, acne, gout, gallstones, edema, eczema, dermatitis, osteoporosis and ulcers.

Routes of application: Apply topically to the bottom of the feet; dilute with an extender oil at three to five drops of wintergreen oil to one Tblsp - add blend to a hand hot bath. Wintergreen oil blends well with basil, birch, cypress, geranium, juniper, lavender, lemongrass, marjoram, peppermint and Roman chamomile oils.

Caution: Pregnant women should consult their physician before use.

Yarrow (*Achillea millefolium*)

Beginning: The yarrow originated in Utah. The legendary Greek hero, Achilles, used yarrow to cure his wounds; the Chinese believe that the fragrance of yarrow allows the meeting of heaven and earth in the Yin and Yang tradition.

Description: The essential oil of yarrow is steam distilled from the flowering top. Key constituents:
Chamazulene (12-19%)
Trans-Beta-Caryophyllene (4-8%)

Germacrene D (4-8%)
Camphor (4-9%)
Sabinene (3-7%)
Beta-Pinene (3-7%)
1,8 Cineol (Eucalyptol) (2-6%)

Therapeutic properties: The essential oil of yarrow is anti-inflammatory, relieves indigestion, scar tissue and enhances wound healing. Yarrow essential oil is a potent decongestant of the prostate gland, balances hormones, relieves acne, dysmenorrhea, anorexia, bladder and kidney weakness, cellulite, respiratory infections, stimulates digestion, eczema, gastritis, gout, alopecia, headaches, hemorrhoids, high blood pressure, menopausal symptoms, neuritis, neuralgia, urinary infections, arthritis, rheumatism, sprains, thrombosis, ulcers, varicose veins, vaginitis and ulcers.

Routes of application: Diffuse or apply topically.

Caution: Pregnant women should consult their physician before use.

Ylang-Ylang (*Cananga odorata*)

Beginnings: Ylang-Ylang is a tropical tree that was historically used to treat malaria, insect bites and infections. The name Ylang-Ylang translates to "flower of flowers" and is known as the "perfume tree," it was used to cover the honeymoon bed of newlyweds. It was revered for its antiseptic, tonic and aphrodisiac properties. The oil extracted from the flowers was mixed with coconut oil to perfume and condition the skin and hair.

Description: Ylang-Ylang is a native of Indonesia, Commores and the Philippines and reaches a height of 60 feet. The yellow flowers are freshly picked in the early morning and the oil is extracted by steam-distillation; the second pass distillation oil is known as "cananga." Key constituents:

Germacrene D (15-20%)

Alpha Farnesene (8-12%)
Benzyl Acetate (9-15%)
Benzyl Benzoate (3-6%)
Linalol (6-10%)
Methyl Paracresol (5-9%)
Isoeugenol (3-5%)
Cinnamyl acetate (3-5%)

Therapeutic properties: Ylang-Ylang essential oil is antispasmodic, typically Ylang-Ylang is used to relieve anxiety, depression, insomnia, hypertension, irregular heart beat, skin conditions and frigidity.

Routes of application: Baths, diffuse and massage. The Ylang-Ylang oil blends well with bergamot, clary sage, *Eucalyptus citriodora*, ginger, grapefruit, jasmine, lemon, litsea cubeba, mandarin, melissa, neroli, palmarosa, patchouli, petitgrain, Roman chamomile, rose, sandalwood and vetiver oils.

Cautions: Pregnant women should consult their physician before use; high concentrations can produce headache and nausea.

Yuzu (*Citrus junos*)

Beginnings: Yuzu was first noted in China in 237 B.C. by Pu-Wei in his book, *Spring and Summer Annals*. The tree is still cultivated in north-central China, however, it is grown more extensively in Japan in modern times. The tree was introduced into Japan 1,000 years ago. Yuzu is cold resistant and is therefore able to be grown in areas unavailable to other citrus varieties. In Japan the rind, juice and fruit are used widely as flavorings in vinegars, soups, seafood dishes, sauces, pickles and salads. It is used by Shinto priests for purification before prayer. It is used as an ingredient for a soft drink popular in South America.

Description: The yuzu is an evergreen, spring fruit tree growing up to 15 feet in height with white flowers and yellow-green fruit. The fruit is low in mass for its size, it has a thick, pithy skin and minimal juice. The essential oil is cold pressed from the rind of the fruit. Key ingredients:

Limonene
Y-Terpinene
B-Phellandrene
Mycene
Linalol
A-Pinene
Terpinolene

Therapeutic properties: The yuzu essential oil has tonic, stimulant, antibiotic, anti-infectious, antiputrescent, diuretic, antiviral, calmative, nervine, sedative, antiseptic, analgesic and antifungal properties; yuzu is used as a general tonic, and to treat nervous tension, stress, anxiety, cystitis, constipation, cleansing, nervous stomach, cramps, neuralgia, post-viral symptoms and convalescence from chronic diseases.

Routes of application: Yuzu blends well with basil, bay, bergamot, black pepper, cardamom, cedarwood, clary sage, clove, coriander, cypress, *Eucalyptus citriodora*, ginger, jasmine, lavender, marjoram, orange, lemon, patchouli, palmarosa, petitgrain, pine, Roman chamomile, ravensara, rose, rosemary, sandalwood, vetiver and ylang-ylang.

Chapter 5

"The Hittites' admiration for Egyptian expertise in herbal medicine (and in the use of essential oils) is corroborated by a text noting that Rameses (II) sent pharmaceutical preparations instead of physicians to Hattusili (the Hittite sovereign), who suffered from ophthalmia."

- from
Medicine in the Days of the Pharaohs

Materia Medica for Essential Oils

The use of essential oils for medicinal purposes was the natural extension of the ancient art of herbal medicine.

The primary sources of information on early Egyptian health practices that used herbs and essential oils are the various medical papyri, ostraca, epigraphic inscriptions, graffiti and works of art which are supplemented by the writings of Greco-Roman antiquity, biblical stories and the modern pathological examination of mummies. The information is often sketchy or patchwork because of serious damage produced to historical writings by the ravages of nature, war and human scavengers over the last five millennia. The classic example of this type of willful destruction of information is the purposeful burning of the great Library of Alexandria, which was reported to have contained as many as 700,000 written works in the time of Queen Cleopatra VII Philopater.

Original Sources of Essential Oil Information

It was not until 1853, however, that Heinrich Brugsch made the first direct translation of a medical papyrus. A second approach to gathering medicinal information consisted of seeking common roots for words in Egyptian, Greek (numerous Greek writers, lead by Dioscorides, used original Greek words for medicinal plants and oils in their lists of medicines), Hebrew (which had bits of Egyptian words in their recorded lists) and Arabic.

According to Thierry Bardinet, "the medial papyri are essentially practical manuals composed to allow a physician to diagnose pathologies in his daily practice and prose a suitable treatment. They are not theoretical treatises in the modern sense of the term - they do not explain illnesses - and, for this reason, a (medical) physician of the twentieth century is likely to find them inaccessible."

The Ebers Papyrus: Currently housed in the library at the University of Leipzig, the Ebers Papyrus is the longest and the most complete of the medical papyri discovered. The name comes from the German scholar, Georg Ebers (1837 - 1898), who had purchased the document in 1872 from an Egyptian who claimed to have found it ten years earlier between the legs of a mummy in a tomb at Thebes. Three years later Ebers published a copy of the papyrus; translations followed - a German version by Walter Wreszinski in 1913 and an English version by Bendix Ebbell in 1937.

The Ebers Papyrus is more than 20 meters long and 30 centimeters wide and consists of 108 pages of 20 - 22 lines each. The text, written in hieratic, dates from about 1500 B.C. during the reign of Amenhotep I. It is thought to be at least a partial copy of an earlier papyrus written in 2300 B.C. It is primarily a compilation of pharmacology and therapeutics (only 47 remedies are directly attached to a description of the disease). Some of its chapters, including the Book of the Heart, are considered to be the most important historical documents of modern medicine because it shows that the concept of "rational" medicine existed much earlier than the time of the Greek physicians.

The Edwin Smith Papyrus: This papyrus is displayed at the New

York Academy of Medicine; it was purchased in 1862 by a novice American Egyptologist by the name of Edwin Smith from a merchant in Luxor by the name of Mustafa Agha. Smith's daughter donated the document to the New York Historical Society in 1906, following his death.

The papyrus was translated by Henry Breasted, director of the Oriental Institute at the University of Chicago - the translation was published in a two volume work in 1930. It is thought to have come from the same tomb in the Theban necropolis as the Ebers Papyrus.

It consists of 12 pages, 4.68 meters in length and 33 centimeters wide and covered with hieratic script. The titles are written in red ink and the main text in black ink. The descriptions start at the top of the head and move down (skull, face, neck, clavicles, shoulders, chest, vertebrae), 48 cases outline traumas of the bone and soft tissues in a very organized form - each observation is listed as a clinical description followed by a diagnosis, prognosis and lastly the treatments to be administered.

The Hearst Papyrus: This papyrus was discovered in 1899 from excavations at Deir el-Ballas; it was acquired two years later by the Hearst Expedition lead into Egypt by George A. Reisner, who published the hieratic text in 1905. A German translation was published by Wreszinski in 1912. The papyrus is currently owned by the University of California. It is thought to have been written during the reign of Thutmose III; it contains 260 paragraphs of medical recipes for treating diseases of the skin, heart, bladder and chest; dental problems; parasitic diseases; the loss and whitening of the hair; bites; and fractures. Many of the Hearst prescriptions are found in the Ebers Papyrus.

The Berlin Papyri: The Berlin Papyrus is stored at the Aegyptisches Museum in Berlin; it contains 204 paragraphs. It was discovered by Giuseppe Passalacqua in a terracotta vase that had been buried ten feet under the sand near Saqqara. It was published in a German edition by Wreszinski in 1909. It is the only "signed" medical text that has survived - "It was the scribe of sacred writings, the chief of excellent physicians, (who made) the book."

Part of a second medical papyrus, also in the museum's collection, referred to as the "small" Berlin Papyrus, consists of 15 pages that contain magical chants for the protection of mothers and children as well as a collection of diseases of infants (it is thought to be the oldest pediatric work known).

A third papyrus, also held in the Berlin Museum, written in demotic in the first century B.C., contains prescriptions for preventing pregnancy.

The Kahun Papyrus: This papyrus is held at University College of London, it was discovered by Sir William Matthew Flinders Petrie in 1889 near the village of Kahun, in the Faiyum, among the ruins of the pharaonic residence at Kahun. Restored and translated by Francis Griffith in 1898 - it is thought to be the oldest medical papyrus that has been found to date; it is dated during the reign of Amenemhat III (approximately 1850 B.C.). It is primarily a study of gynecology and obstetrics with a section describing veterinary medicine (written in hieroglyphics).

The London Medical Papyrus: This papyrus was acquired by the British Museum in 1860 from the Royal Institution of London and translated into German by Wrenszinski in 1912. Dating from 1350 B.C., dated during the reign of Tutankhamum, and measuring 1.25 meters in length and 17.5 centimeters wide, it is a collection of magical formulas containing 63 prescriptions for the treatment of diseases of the eyes, gynecological problems and burns.

The Chester Beatty Papyrus VI: This papyrus, dating from 1300 B.C., is thought to have been copied from an earlier papyrus; it was part of a cache of documents discovered during excavations of Deir el-Medina that were eventually stored in England, Ireland and Egypt. The recto is a collection of diseases of the anus; the vero contains formulae for disorders of the breasts, heart, and bladder as well as incantations.

The Magical Papyri of Leiden: These two papyri were discovered at Thebes and are currently held at the University Museum of Leiden.

They are dated from the 18th and 19th Dynasties. Both are thought to be copies of older texts that primarily contain remedies and magical formulas against numerous conditions.

A separate text dating from the third century A.D., the Demotic Magical Papyrus of London and Leiden, was translated into English by Griffith and Thompson in 1904.

The Brooklyn Papyrus: These two documents (Brooklyn Museum) dating from the 30th Dynasty (350 B.C.), make up a single papyrus devoted to herpetology and ophiology. It describes various reptiles and the results of their bites and describes methods of treatment.

The Carlsberg Papyrus VIII: This papyrus is of unknown origin was first published for the first time in 1939, in English, by Erick Iversen. Three fragments, written in hieratic, are dated from the 19th and 20th Dynasties. The document is held at the Egyptological Institute of the University of Copenhagen; it is mainly made up of gynecological prescriptions and information on pregnancy.

The Ramesseum Papyri III, IV and V: These papyri, published by Alan Gardiner in 1955, were originally discovered in 1896 by James Quibell in a tomb of the Middle Kingdom near the Ramesseum. Papyrus III deals with ocular diseases and illnesses of children; IV, illnesses of women and children; and V, vascular diseases. They contain mixed medical and magical information, except for V which is purely medical in nature.

Other Papyri: A number of papyri are either partly or completely medical. These include the Amherst Papyrus; the Cairo Papyrus; the Anastasi papyrus; the Insinger Papyrus, an important Late Period demotic, wisdom text, that covers the nature of God and human morality; the Louvre Papyrus which contains remedies for vascular diseases and hefat-worms; the Westcar Papyrus that describes childbirth; the Vatican Papyrus that contains anatomical lists; and the Vienna Papyrus (also known as the Crocodilopolis Medical Book, a demotic manuscript from the second century A.D., that contains a comprehensive pharmacopoeia.

Essential oils, a subcategory of herbs, are plant medicines that have a long and illustrious history for the relief and elimination of human and animal suffering. They can effectively kill microbes, and reduce or eliminate symptoms of many physical and mental conditions.

Many essential oils were given GRAS status (Generally Regarded as Safe) by the FDA. Essential oils have been used for medicinal purposes for thousands of years by many cultures and as a result, recommendations can be given for their use based on their experiences, observations and writings.

While essential oils can be used to relieve the symptoms of many diseases, to ensure optimal benefit from the use of essential oils as a home remedy or clinical therapeutic agent, essential oils are not panaceas, therefore, it is sometimes necessary and prudent to add them to the appropriate nutritional regimes and medical therapies.

Table 5-1. Essential Oils on the GRAS List

Angelica	Lemongrass
Basil	Lime
Bergamot	*Melaleuca alternifolia*
Cedarwood	Melissa (lemon balm)
Celery seed	Mandarin
Chamomile, Roman	Marjoram
Chamomile, German	Myrrh
Cinnamon bark	Myrtle
Cistus	Neroli
Citrus rinds (all varieties)	Nutmeg
Citronella	Orange
Clary Sage	Oregano
Clove	Palmarosa
Coriander	Patchouli
Cumin	Pepper
Dill	Peppermint
Elemi	Petitgrain
Eucalyptus globulus	Pine
Fennel	Rosemary
Fir	Rose
Frankincense	Rosewood
Galbanum	Sage
Geranium	Savory
Ginger	Sandalwood
Grapefruit	Spearmint
Helichrysum	Spikenard
Hyssop	Spruce
Jasmine	Tangerine
Juniper	Tarragon
Laurus nobilis	Thyme
Lavandin	Valerian
Lavender	Vetiver
Lemon	Ylang Ylang

Use Codes

A	Apply topically to the affected area directly, carefully, without stimulating or moving it.
B	Bath
C	Compress
CB	Cotton bud
DS	Dressing
FO	Face oil
FB	Foot bath
FM	Face mask
FT	Face tonic
G	Gauze
GR	Gargle
HDIL	High dilution
I	Inhalation: water bowl, inhalation from bottle or tissue
LC	Lotions and creams
M	Massage
MW	Mouthwash
N	Neat
R	Apply gently "rub"
RF	Room fragrance, diffused
S	Spray
SB	Sitz bath
ST	Scalp treatment
W	Wash

Worwood, S. and Worwood, V. A.: essential aromatherapy. New World Library. 2003.

There are general guidelines and common sense restrictions required for the safe and effective use of essential oils for home remedies. Essential oils should be used diluted with carrier oils unless otherwise noted.

Essential oils to be avoided or used only under the care and direction of an expert:

Sensitive skin:
Basil, birch, black pepper, cinnamon, clove, cumin, fennel, fir, ginger, lemon, lemongrass, lemon verbena, oregano, parsley seed, peppermint, pimento berry, pine, tagetes, red thyme, wintergreen.

Prior to exposure to sunlight:
Angelica, bergamot, cumin, grapefruit, lemon, lemon verbena, lime, orange, yuzu, tangerine, mandarin.

Babies and children:
Use only essential oils specifically recommended for babies and children.

Driving (avoid scenting vehicle while operating vehicle):
carnation, Roman chamomile, geranium, hops, hyacinth, lavender, linden blossom, mace, marjoram, neroli, nutmeg, ormenis flower, petitgrain, rose, sandalwood, spikenard, valerian, vetiver, ylang-ylang.

Epilepsy:
Fennel, hyssop, rosemary, sage, wormwood.

Hypertension:
Hyssop, rosemary, sage, thyme.

Kidney or liver disease*:
Fennel, juniper berry (people with liver disease should take extra caution when considering the use of essential oils).

Clothing (essential oils can stain or damage):
Velvet, silk.

Furniture (essential oils can damage the surface finish):
Wood furniture, polished furniture.

Flammable:
Do not store or use near, heat, flame or electrical outlets.

Do Not Use For Aromatherapy Under Any Circumstances*:
Bitter almond, boldo leaf, calamus, yellow camphor, horseradish, jaborandi leaf, mugwort, mustard, pennyroyal, rue, sassafras, savin, southernwood, Idaho tansy, thuja, wintergreen, warmseed, wormwood.

---

*International Federation of Aromatherapists

Classical Uses of Essential Oils for Aromatherapy

Abdomen R, M

Bloated

Fennel, cardamom, peppermint

Gas	Fennel, coriander, peppermint	R, M
Colic (adult)	Roman chamomile, cardamom, coriander, peppermint, fennel, ginger, juniper.	R, M
Pain	black pepper, *Eucalyptus radiata*, Lavender, fennel, ginger, cardamom, peppermint, ravensara.	R, M, B
Cramp	black pepper, Roman chamomile, clary sage, coriander, lavender, peppermint, Yuzu.	R, M, B
Abscess		
External		
Dry	Lavender, manuka, ravensara, tea tree *Melaleuca alternifolia*, Oregano and lavender, Frankincense and lavender, 1st Defense.	A, G, C, N,R
Weeping	Bergamot, frankincense, lavender, manuka, tea tree, ravensara	A, G, C, N, W
Breast	Bergamot, lavender, manuka, ravensara	A, C, G, N, W, HDL
Abscess		
Mouth	Manuka, tea tree, *Melaleuca alternifolia*, myrrh; 1st Defense	MW, CB
Abscess		
Dental	Roman chamomile, German chamomile, manuka, tea tree	MW, CB

Absentmindedness

Peppermint, cardamom, vetiver, frankincense, sandalwood, rosemary, basil, pine, lemon; Awareness.

Abuse (mental or physical)

Geranium, sandalwood, melissa, lavender; To Be Loved, To Be at Peace, Robe of Light, Trauma, To Be Happy, 1st Defense.

Acid/Alkaline Balance

Clove to relieve acid conditions.

Acidosis

Peppermint, lemon, clove.

Acne

General	Bergamot, cedarwood, German chamomile, *Eucalyptus radiata*, geranium, grapefruit, juniper, lavender, lemon, lemongrass, *Litsea cubeba*, palmarosa, petigrain, ravensara, rosemary, sandalwood, tea tree, thyme; oregano and lavender.	FO, CB, S, W
Red	Roman chamomile, German chamomile, *Eucalyptus radiata*, geranium, juniper, lavender.	FO CB S, W
Pustule	Bergamot, lemon, tea tree, thyme, rosemary.	FO, CB, S
Scarring	Frankincense, palmarosa, petitgrain.	FO, S, W

ADD

Lemon, lavender, Roman chamomile, mandarin; To Be at Peace, To Be Happy.

Addictions	Roman chamomile, clary sage, bergamot, jasmine, juniper, lavender, ylang-ylang, yuzu, frankincense; To Be at Peace, Robe of Light.	B, M RF

Addison's Disease

Geranium, rosemary, sage, lavender, peppermint, ravensara, thyme; To Be at Peace, To Be Well.

Adenoids

Enlarged

Cypress, juniper, *Eucalyptus radiata,* tea tree.	GR, MW, M

Pus-covered

Clove, *Eucalyptus radiata*, manuka, tea tree.	GR MW M

Adrenal Imbalance or Exhaustion

Nutmeg, clove, rosemary, basil, ravensara, peppermint, thyme, geranium, lavender, Roman chamomile; Sage and Nutmeg,

Cushing's Disease

Lemon

Agent Orange		
	Ledum, German chamomile, carrot seed oil, helichrysum; To Be Well.	
Aging	Geranium, jasmine, ginger, neroli, rose, rosemary, thyme, yuzu.	M, B R, I
Agitation		
	Lavender, orange, Roman chamomile, bergamot, ylang-ylang, neroli, geranium, jasmine, melissa, marjoram, cypress, sandalwood, mandarin; To Be at Peace.	
AIDS (HIV)		
	Cistus, lemon, cumin, myrrh, blue cypress, lemon, ravensara, thyme, basil, germanium; 1st Defense, Deep Cleanser, Awareness, To Be at Peace, GI Purify.	
Alcoholism		
	Lavender, Roman chamomile, orange, helichrysum, elemi, bergamot, jasmine, ylang-ylang, frankincense, Roman chamomile, clove, *Rosemary verbenon*; To Be at Peace, Robe of Light.	
Alkalosis		
	Ginger, tarragon, anise; GI Purify.	
Allergies		
	Lavender, ledum, Roman chamomile, neroli, peppermint, helichrysum, patchouli, ravensara, *Tanacetum annum*; lavender and frankincense, 1st Defense.	B, M I, RF

Alopecia

Thyme, rosemary, lavender, cedarwood,	M, R
clary sage, cypress.	W

Alzheimer's Disease

Ginger, rose, lavender, pine, *Eucalyptus radiata*, basil, rosemary, peppermint, vanilla; To Be at Peace, To Be Happy, To Be Well, To Be Loved.

Analgesia

Black pepper, Roman chamomile,	M, B
helichrysum, yuzu, elemi, winter	C.G
green/birch, clove, peppermint, lavender,	
lemongrass.	

Anemia

Lemon

Aneurysm

Helichrysum, sandalwood, cypress.

Anorexia

To relax

Bergamot, tarragon, mandarin, orange,	B
lemon, Roman chamomile, clary sage,	M
lavender, neroli, palmarosa, ginger.	I, RF

App./Stimulant

Black pepper, cardamom, coriander,	I
fennel.	RF

Strengthening

Cardamom, ginger, lemon, *Litsea*	I
cubeba, rosemary.	RF
	B, M

Anthrax

Thyme, oregano, clove, cinnamon, rosewood; 1st Defense.

Skin

Oregano and lavender.

Ihalation

Lemon; To Be Well.

Antiseptic

Rosemary, manuka, blue cypress, *Rosemary verbenon*, thyme, *Eucalyptus globulus*, *E. radiata*, , mountain savory, *Melaleuca alternifolia*, lavandin, lemon, pine, lemongrass, clove, cinnamon, oregano; Deep Cleanser, 1st Defense, GI Purity, To Be Well, Lavender and frankincense

Apnea (sleep)

Ravensara, thyme linalol; Awareness.

Appetite

Loss

Basil, cardamom, coriander, fennel, rosemary, ginger, lemon, orange; GI Purity. R, M S

Suppressed

Bergamot, ginger, spearmint, orange or nutmeg. RF I

Arteriosclerosis

Helichrysum, juniper berry, cypress, frankincense.

Arthritis (Osteoarthritis)

General

Wintergreen/birch, helichrysum, fir, spruce, pine, cypress, peppermint, vetiver, marjoram, rosemary, *Eucalyptus citriodora*, *E. globulus*, *E. radiata*, basil, oregano, lemongrass, black pepper, elemi, tea tree, lavender, lemon, thyme, myrtle, myrrh, *Melaleuca alternifolia*; Trauma,	M, R C, B

Redness

Roman chamomile, German	M, R

Swelling

Chamomile, juniper, lavender.	C, B

Pain

Black pepper, Roman chamomile, cypress, ginger, helichrysum, lavender, rosemary.	M, R C, B

Asthma

Cedarwood, German chamomile, cypress, *Eucalyptus globulus, E. radiata, E. citriodora*, frankincense, lavender, marjoram, neroli, pine, rose, yuzu; Breath of Life, To Be Well, lavender and frankincense.	M, R B, I RF

Lavender, Roman chamomile, *Eucalyptus polybractea*, myrtle, peppermint, frankincense, marjoram or rose.

Frankincense with ravensara, cypress, fir, spruce, pine, lemon, thyme, rosemary, *Eucalyptus radiata*, helichrysum, wintergreen/birch or myrtle.

Rosemary, ravensara, *Eucalyptus radiata*, mountain savory, lemon or juniper berries.

Sage with lavender, myrrh. Hyssop or *Eucalyptus radiata*.

Athlete's Foot

Lavender, manuka, myrrh, palmarosa, patchouli, tagetes, *Melaleuca alternifolia*, cypress; Oregano and lavender. — FB, N, CB

Attention Deficit Disorder (ADD)

Lavender, sandalwood, cardamom, basil, frankincense, ledum, vetiver, lemon, Roman chamomile, mandarin; To Be Happy, To Be at Peace.

Autism

Frankincense, sandalwood, melissa, lavender, *Basil eugeno,* geranium, vetiver, rose, ylang-ylang; To Be Loved, To Be at Peace, Awareness, Robe of Light, Lavender and frankincense.

Babies

Colic	Lavender, Roman chamomile.	M, R
Colds & Coughs	*Eucalyptus radiata*, frankincense, tea tree.	M, R B, RF
Cradle cap	Lavender, tea tree.	M, R

Earache		
	Roman chamomile, tea tree.	M, R
Minor Discomforts		
	Lavender, Roman chamomile, Mandarin.	M, R B
Diaper rash		
	Roman chamomile, lavender, manuka, tea tree.	C, G, B, R, HDIL
Sleeplessness		
	Roman chamomile, lavender, Neroli.	RF, M, R B
Teething	Roman chamomile	R,M (outer jaw massage)
Post natal depression		
	Bergamot, Roman chamomile, jasmine, neroli, linden blossom, rose, yuzu.	B, M R, RF FO, S

Back injuries and pain

Basil, black pepper, Roman chamomile, clary sage, cypress, ginger, helichrysum, marjoram, oregano, peppermint, rosemary, spikenard, thyme, lavender, birch, *Eucalyptus citriodora*; Trauma.	M, B R

Bacterial infection

Melaleuca alternifolia

Baldness

Lavender, *Litsea cubeba*, jojoba, rosemary, cypress.

Bed sores

Bergamot, lavender, frankincense, manuka, ravensara, tea tree, yazu. — A, C / G, CB / HDIL

Bed-Wetting

Roman chamomile, lavender, mandarin, petitgrain, cypress, juniper berry, sandalwood; To Be Well. — B, M / RF

Belching

Cardamom, coriander, fennel, ginger. — I, M / RF

Bell's Palsy

Ravensara, thyme linalol.

Bites
(Insect bites)

Animal

Bergamot, lavender, lemon, manuka, Oregano, helichrysum, tea tree, thyme. — A, N / CB, G / W, DS

Insect

Eucalyptus globulus, *Ecalyptus radiata*, lavender, lemon, manuka, patchouli, tea tree. — A, N / CB, G / W, DS

Bee sting

Patchouli, thyme linalol; Lavender and frankincense.

Spider

Brown recluse

Oregano and Lavender

Black widow

Patchouli, thyme linalol, *Eucalyptus citriodora.*

Human	Bergamot, lavender, helichrysum, oregano, tea tree, thyme.	A, N CB, G W, DS
Reptile	Clove, lavender, oregano, tea tree, thyme.	A, N CG, G W, DS

Black eye

Lavender	C

Bladder Infection

Sandalwood, *Melaleuca alternifolia*; 1st Defense.	B, SB M

Bleeding

Cypress, helichrysum, lavender, geranium, cistus.

Bleeding Gums

Melaleuca alternifolia, myrrh.

Blisters

Melaleuca alternifolia, lavender, melissa,	C, DS

cistus, geranium, myrrh, tagetes, tea tree, yuzu. G, CB

Bloating

Tarragon, peppermint, juniper berry, fennel; GI Purify.

Blood Clots (Embolism, thrombosis)

Helichrysum, clove, lemon, orange, grapefruit, tangerine, cypress.

Blood disorders (Anemia)

Lemon, lemongrass, spikenard, helichrysum.

Blood Detoxifacation

Helichrysum, German chamomile, Roman chamomile, *Rosemary verbenon,* geranium; lemon, orange or cardamom.

Blood Oxygenation

Helichrysum, lemongrass, pepper, spruce, anise.

Blood Pressure (High)

Marjoram, rosemary, clary sage, mandarin, helichrysum, Roman chamomile, lavender, frankincense, ylang-ylang,; To Be at Peace, To Be Happy.

Lavender, ylang-ylang, marjoram, cypress, mountain savory or helichrysum.

Rosemary, ylang-ylang, marjoram, helichrysum or lavender.

Blood Pressure (Low)

Sage, pine, rosemary, thyme, mandarin, peppermint, lemon, cypress, frankincense, ravensara, juniper berry.

Body odor

Bergamot, clary sage, cypress, geranium, juniper, lemon.	R, B M, S W

Boils

Bergamot, Frankincense, lavender, Roman, German chamomile, patchouli, myrrh, juniper, lemon, *Litsea cubeba*, tea tree, thyme, ravensara, *Melaleuca alternifolia*, yuzu; Frankincense and lavender, Oregano and lavender.	C, G W, N CB, HDIL

Bone Ache

Wintergreen/birch, birch, spruce, pine.

Bone Trauma (Bruises, fractures, calcium deposits, spurs)

Wintergreen/birch, spruce, fir, pine, cypress, peppermint, rosemary, basil or elemi; Trauma.

Cypress, spruce, fir, pine, cedarwood, rosemary, peppermint, helichrysum, wintergreen/birch, basil, lemongrass, clove or ginger.

Bowel Disorders

Inflammation

Roman chamomile, German chamomile, cypress, lavender, *Litsea cubeba*, patchouli, peppermint.	M, R C, B

Pain

Cypress, fennel, helichrysum, peppermint.	M, R C, B

Discomfort

Helichrysum, patchouli, peppermint.	M, R C, B

Swelling

Cypress, fennel, juniper.	M, R C, B

Brain Disorders

Cedarwood, vetiver, sandalwood, black pepper, patchouli, myrrh, ginger, vitex, German chamomile, spikenard, galbanum, frankincense, melissa, helichrysum; Awareness.

Breath (Bad)

Clove, lavender, peppermint, tea tree.	MW, G

Breathing Difficulties

Cedarwood, *Eucalyptus globulus*, *Eucalyptus radiata*, pine, ravensara.	I, B M, R

Bronchitis

General

Cypress, rosemary, lemon, cinnamon, *Eucalyptus radiata*, frankincense, marjoram, sandalwood, ravensara, thyme, wintergreen/birch, myrrh, dill, fir, spruce, pine, oregano, helichrysum, rose, neroli *Melaleuca alternifolia*, clove, lavender, spearmint, clary sage, hyssop, ledum, myrtle, Douglas firs, white fir; Breath of Life, 1st Defense, To Be Well.	I, B RF M, R

Acute

Cinnamon, *Eucalyptus globulus*, ravensara, thyme.	I, B RF, M, R

Chronic

Eucalyptus radiata, pine, ravensara.	I, B RF M, R

Cough

Cypress, ravensara, sandalwood, cedarwood; lavender and frankincense, Breath of Life.	I, B RF M, R

Congestion

Eucalyptus globulus, *Eucalyptus radiata*, frankincense, helichrysum, tea tree, thyme, ravensara.	I, B RF M, R

Bruising

Cypress, helichrysum, lavender, white fir, fennel, geranium, rosemary, tea tree, amyris; Trauma.	N, C G, DS

Bunions

German chamomile, marjoram, peppermint, tagetes.	CB, M R, FB

Burns

Lavender (with peppermint -1 drop diluted in ten drops of lavender), blue cypress; lemon, lavender.	N, G DS

Bursitis

Marjoram, basil, lavender, pepper, spruce, fir, pine, peppermint, clary sage, cypress, juniper, ginger, wintergreen/birch, elemi, rosemary, helichrysum; Trauma.	M, R C

Cancer

Helichrysum, lemon, orange, myrrh, tangerine, lavender, clove, white fir, tsuga, frankincense; 1st Defense.

Candida

Manuka, melissa, tea tree.	SB, M B, R

Mouth thrush

Manuka, melissa, tea tree.	MW GR

Canker Sores

Melissa, sandalwood, *Melaleuca quienquenervia.*

Carbuncle

Cypress, lavender, ravensara, thyme. CB, C

Cardiovascular Diseases

Elevated Cholesterol

Rosemary, clove, Roman chamomile, spikenard, *Helichrysum italicum*.

Arteriosclerosis

Helichrysum, cypress.

Phlebitis

German chamomile, nutmeg, Roman chamomile, *Amyris balsamifera*, geranium.

Tachycardia (rapid heart rate)

Ylang-ylang.

Car Sickness

Ginger, peppermint.

I

Carpal Tunnel Syndrome

Lavender, marjoram, birch, *Melaleuca alternifolia*, basil, Roman chamomile; Trauma.

Catarrh

Cedarwood, *Eucalyptus radiata*, M, R
frankincense, myrrh, peppermint, I, B
rosemary, sandalwood, tea tree.

Cellulite

Rosemary, grapefruit, basil, lemon, cypress, fennel, juniper, spearmint, tangerine, lemongrass, cedarwood, *Litsea cubeba*, pine, rosemary, bitter orange.	M, R B

Chemical Sensitivity

Frankincense and Sandalwood.

Chicken Pox

Lavender, blue cypress, bergamot, sandalwood, Roman chamomile, *Melaleuca quienquenervia*, melissa, German chamomile, *Eucalyptus radiata*, *Litsea cubeba*, ravensara, tea tree; To Be Well.	A, W C, G, S

Chilblains

German and Roman chamomile, cypress *Eucalyptus globulus*, *Eucalyptus radiata*, geranium, juniper, lavender, lemon, marjoram, rosemary.	N, CB C, G R

Chills

Black pepper, ginger, cinnamon, clove, geranium.	M, R

Cholera

Clove, ravensara, rosemary, sage, thyme; 1st Defense.

Chronic Fatigue Syndrome

Rosemary, *Melaleuca alternifolia*, thyme, nutmeg, basil, peppermint, ginger, ravensara; 1st Defense, Awareness.

Circulation Disorders

Helichrysum, bay, black pepper, frankincense, marjoram, cypress, myrtle, lemon, peppermint, orange, grapefruit, goldenrod, clove, rose, rosemary, thyme, ginger; Trauma. M, R B

Cold Sores (Herpes Simplex Type 1)

Melissa, *Eucalyptus citriodora*, blue cypress, *Melaleuca quienquenervia*, geranium, sandalwood, manuka, ravensara, tea tree, yuzu. N, CB

Colds and Flu

Lavender, lemon, lemongrass, Roman and German chamomile, marjoram, bay, black pepper, ginger, tarragon, manuka, cedarwood, peppermint, myrrh, orange, pine, ravensara, oregano, frankincense, thyme, fennel or *Laurus nobilis,* basil, clove, *Eucalyptus globulus*, *E. radiata*, rosemary, tea tree, thyme; Breath of Life, lavender and frankincense. I, M R, B

Congestion

Ledum, western red cedar, wintergreen/ birch, frankincense, white fir, lemon, pine; Breath of Life, 1st Defense, To Be Well.

Coughs

Myrtle, goldenrod, ledum, fir, ravensara, cedarwood; Breath of Life, lavender and frankincense.

Flu-like

Goldenrod, melissa, orange, oregano, ravensara, thyme.

Laryngitis

Melaleuca alternifolia; 1st Defense, To Be Well.

Colitis (Ulcerative)

Peppermint, spearmint, tarragon, anise seed, fennel, patchouli, rosemary, cinnamon, clove; 1st Defense. M, R

Colitis (viral)

Blue cypress, melissa, Melaleuca alternifolia, thyme, cinnamon, clove; 1st Defense. M, R

Coma

Frankincense, vetiver, sandalwood, ylang-ylang, cypress, pepper, peppermint, basil; Awareness, Robe of Light.

Confusion

Peppermint, lemon, rosemary, basil, cardamom, vetiver; Awareness.

Congestion (Sinus)

Sandalwood, white fir, western red cedar, coriander, cypress, *Eucalyptus radiata*, I, RF

Melaleuca alternifolia, peppermint, fennel, rosemary, ravensara, myrtle, basil, bay, ginger; Breath of Life.

Congestive Heart Failure

Helichrysum, cypress, goldenrod.

Connective Tissue (Sprains, Strains and Tendonitis)

Basil, lemongrass, lavender, marjoram, helichrysum, wintergreen/birch; Trauma.

Bone

Wintergreen/birch, spruce, fir; Trauma.

Muscle

Basil, marjoram, lavender; Trauma.

Ligament

Lemongrass, lavender; Trauma.

Tendons

Lavender, lemongrass, marjoram; Trauma.

Constipation

Ginger, black pepper, peppermint, fennel, tarragon, cardamom, mandarin, orange, patchouli, rosemary, yuzu, anise seed, marjoram; GI Purity. M, R B

Corns

Lemon, tagetes, peppermint, *Melaleuca alternifolia*, myrrh; Oregano and lavender, 1st Defense. N, CB FB

Coughs

Black pepper, cardamom, cedarwood, cypress, *Eucalyptus globulus*, *E. radiata*, fennel, frankincense, helichrysum, lemon, marjoram, myrrh, peppermint, pine, rosemary, sandalwood, tagetes, thyme.	R, I RF

Cramps (Abdominal)

Clary sage, cypress, geranium, juniper, marjoram, orange, peppermint, lavender; GI Purity.	M, R B

Cramps (Muscle)

Geranium, marjoram, rosemary, birch, lavender, *Melaleuca alternifolia*, black pepper, peppermint, helichrysum; Trauma, lavender and frankincense.	M, R B

Crohn's Disease

Peppermint, cinnamon, clove, 1st Defense.

Cushing's Disease (Adrenal Gland Failure)

Lavender, Roman chamomile, rosemary, ravensara, peppermint, thyme, geranium, lemon.

Cuts

Lavender, tea tree.	N, G DS

Cyst

Thyme, *Litsea cubeba*, yuzu, *Melaleuca alternifolia*; 1st Defense.	N, CB R, C

Cystitis

Bergamot, Roman chamomile, cedarwood, cajeput, *Melaleuca alternifolia*, cypress, frankincense, juniper, ravensara, sandalwood, tea tree, thyme; frankincense and lavender.	MR B SB

Dandruff

Melaleuca alternifolia, cedarwood, lavender, white fir, western red cedar, rosemary, manuka, patchouli, sage, tea tree; Shaman's Blend.	ST W, M

Decongestants

Rosemary, *Eucalyptus globulus*, *E. radiata*; Breath of Life, 1st Defense, To Be Well.

Dental Infections

Bay, clove, myrrh, tea tree.	MW

Dental Pain

Wintergreen/birch, helichrysum, *Melaleuca alternifolia*, *Eucalyptus radiata*, clove, thyme, myrrh and oregano.	MW

Deodorant

Lavender, manuka, geranium, bergamot, cypress, blue cypress, *Eucalyptus globulus, E. radiata, Melaleuca alternifolia*, myrtle; To Be Well.

Depression

Bergamot, Jasmine, lemon, orange, mandarin, clary sage, geranium, sage, frankincense; To Be Happy, To Be Loved, frank incense and Lavender, Robe of Light.

Dermatitis (Eczema)

Lavender, Juniper, ledum, citrus, hystrix, *Apium graveolens*, cistus, German chamomile, geranium, patchouli, *Melaleuca alternifolia*.

Diabetes (Type 2)

Coriander, cinnamon, fennel, dill, cypress, rosemary, pine, ylang-ylang.

Digestive Upset (Diarrhea, Constipation, Intestinal Infections)

Gastrointestinal Complaints

Goldenrod, basil with tarragon, peppermint, fennel, juniper, ginger, geranium, cumin, black pepper.

Gas and flatulence

Peppermint, tarragon, nutmeg, anise seed, fennel, ledum, carrot seed oil; GI Purify.

Cramps (Stomach)

Rosemary, ginger, marjoram; GI Purify.

Detoxification of intestines

Helichrysum, tangerine, ginger, peppermint, B,R
tarragon, lemon, grapefruit, marjoram, M
rosemary; GI Purify.

Diarrhea

Peppermint, cinnamon, clove, nutmeg, orange, black pepper, *Eucalyptus citriodora*, ravensara, *Melaleuca alternifolia*; GI Purify. M, R

Heartburn (Reflux)

Lemon, peppermint, German chamomile, clove, marjoram.

Hiccups

Tarragon.

Indigestion

Peppermint, nutmeg, tarragon, sage, marjoram, orange, tangerine, grapefruit seed oil; GI Purify.

Diphtheria

Goldenrod; 1st Defense, To Be Well, Frankincense and lavender.

Disinfectant

Eucalyptus globulus, *Melaleuca alternifolia*; Deep Cleanser, 1st Defense, To Be Well, Oregano and lavender.

Diuretic

Black pepper, cypress, fennel, juniper, M, R
lemongrass, orange, sandalwood. B

Diverticulosis

Patchouli, anise seed, tarragon, rosemary, fennel, peppermint, mountain savory, oregano, thyme; GI Purify.

Dizziness

Ginger, cypress, tangerine, peppermint, basil, clove, Roman chamomile, cardamom, lavender, vetiver; Awareness.

Dysentary

Lemon, mountain savory, oregano, peppermint, cinnamon, clove, *Eucalyptus citriodora*, ginger, ravensara, *Melaleuca alternifolia*, sandalwood, myrrh; GI Purify.

Ear Infection (Otitis Media)

Thyme, German chamomile, lavender, German chamomile, *Melaleuca alternifolia*; Trauma. C, M R

Ear Mites

Eucalyptus radiata or Melaleuca alternifolia.

Eczema

Bergamot, German or Roman chamomile, geranium, juniper, lavender, palmarosa, patchouli, sandalwood; Lavender and frankincense. A, C R, B G, C

Edema

Cypress, fennel, juniper berries, lemongrass, sandalwood.

Emotional Trauma

Balsam fir, frankincense, lavender, orange, tangerine, lemon, German chamomile, cypress, patchouli, sandalwood, myrrh, juniper, rose, galbanum, geranium, helichrysum, neroli; Trauma, Robe of Light, To Be Loved, To Be at Peace.

Emotional State

Anxiety

Bergamot, cedarwood, Roman chamomile, clary sage, *Eucalyptus citriodora*, jasmine, lavender, *Litsea cubeba*, marjoram, neroli, patchouli, petitgrain, rose, sandalwood, spikenard, ylang-ylang, yuzu.	B, I M, R RF

Calming

Bay, bergamot, carnation, Roman chamomile, clary sage, *Eucalyptus citriodora*, hyacinth, lavender, mandarin, marjoram, melissa, neroli, petitgrain, rose, sandalwood, vetiver, ylang-ylang, yuzu.	B, I M, R RF

Concentration (Lack of)

Basil, black pepper, cardamom, ginger.	B, I, R, M RF

Depression

Bergamot, carnation, Roman chamomile, clary sage, frankincense, geranium, grapefruit, jasmine, lavender, lemon, *Litsea cubeba*, melissa, neroli, patchouli, petitgrain, rose, sandalwood, ylang-ylang, yuzu.	B, I M, R RF

Emotional crisis

Bergamot, hyacinth, rose.

Fear

Bergamot, Roman chamomile, frankincense, ginger, lavender, neroli, spikenard. — B, M / I, R / RF

Hysteria

Bergamot, Roman chamomile, lavender, melissa, spikenard.

Irritability

Roman chamomile, clary sage, geranium, Lavender, neroli, mandarin, marjoram, petitgrain, sandalwood, vetiver, ylang-ylang.

Mental Exhaustion

Basil, *Eucalyptus citriodora*, *E. globulus*, *E. radiata*, grapefruit, juniper berries, lemon, pine, yuzu.

Nervousness

Roman chamomile, clary sage, cypress, geranium, jasmine, lavender, lemongrass, *Litsea cubeba*, neroli, palmarosa, rose, vetiver, ylang-ylang.

Relaxing

Bergamot, carnation, Roman chamomile, clary sage, *Eucalyptus citriodora*, geranium, hyacinth, jasmine, lavender, *Litsea cubeba*, neroli, palmarosa, petitgrain, rose, sandalwood, vetiver, ylang-ylang.

Shock

Lavender, neroli, rose.

Sorrow

Hyacinth, rose.

Stress

Basil, bergamot, carnation, Roman chamomile, clary sage, clove, frankincense, geranium, hyacinth, jasmine, lavender, lemon, *Litsea cubeba*, mandarin, marjoram, melissa, neroli, palmarosa, patchouli, petitgrain, rose, sandalwood, vetiver, ylang-ylang, yuzu.

Tension

Bergamot, Roman chamomile, cypress, frankincense, geranium, hyacinth, jasmine, lavender, mandarin, marjoram, neroli, petitgrain, rose, sandalwood, spikenard, vetiver, ylang-ylang.

Emphysema

Lemon, lavender, ravensara, *Eucalyptus radiata, Melaleuca alternifolia*; Breath of Life, 1st Defense, To Be Well.

Endocrine System

Helichrysum, *Lippia citriodora*, nutmeg, clove, rosemary, bergamot, spearmint, melissa, spruce, black pepper, geranium, lavender, thyme, peppermint, ravensara; To Be At Peace, To Be Well.

Energy (Lack of)

Lemongrass, juniper, basil, nutmeg, pepper, geranium, rosemary, Roman chamomile, melissa, ylang-ylang, cypress, patchouli, thyme, grapefruit, lemon, orange, ravensara; Awareness, 1st Defense.

B, M, R, RF

Epilepsy (Seizures)

Clary sage, jasmine, ylang-ylang.

Epstein-Barr Syndrome or Virus

Cinnamon, clove, geranium, lemon, melissa, rosemary, ravensara, balsam fir, *Melaleuca alternifolia*; 1st Defense, To Be Well, Oregano and lavender.

Exhaustion (Physical fatigue)

Mountain savory, black pepper, cardamom, clary sage, frankincense, grapefruit, lemon, marjoram, orange, mandarin, palmarosa, petitgrain, rosemary, spikenard, thyme, vetiver, basil, peppermint, ravensara, ylang-ylang; 1st Defense.

B, M
RF,
R

Eye Disorders

Blocked tear ducts

One drop of lavender on bridge of nose.

Cataracts and Glaucoma

Lemongrass, lemon, cypress or *Eucalyptus radiata*.

Drooping Eyelids

Lavender and helichrysum.

Inflamed Eyes

Lavender or lemon.

Blurred Vision

Helichrysum, lavender, peppermint.

* Do Not Use Oils Directly in The Eyes

Fainting

Melissa, peppermint, sandalwood, cardamom, spearmint, basil, lavender rosemary; Trauma, Awareness.	I, RF

Fatigue (Mental)

Basil, bay, coriander, *Eucalyptus citriodora*, pepper, sage, peppermint, geranium, lavender, lemon, *Litsea cubeba*, marjoram, pine, palmarosa, rosemary, nutmeg; Awareness.	B, M RF, R

Feet

Sweaty

Cypress, clary sage, *Eucalyptus globulus*, *E. radiata*, *E. citriodora*, geranium, peppermint, tea tree.	B, FB M, R

Deodorant

Clary sage, juniper berries, lemon.	FB, M, R

Tired

Eucalyptus citriodora, rosemary, Peppermint.	FB M, R

Fertility

Clary sage, sage, anise seed, fennel, yarrow, geranium, bergamot, rose.

Fever

Ledum, white fir, bergamot, black pepper, lavender, peppermint, *Eucalyptus radiata*, *E. globulus*, ginger, lemon, melissa, ravensara, tea tee, sandalwood, German and Roman chamomile, rosemary.	C, I RF, R

Fibroids

Frankincense, *Inula graveolens*, cistus, lavender, oregano, pine and helichrysum.

Fibromyalgia

Douglas fir, white fir, balsam fir, peppermint, Helichrysum, rosemary, ravensara, thyme; Trauma.

Flatulence (bowel)

Peppermint, fennel, cardamom, coriander, spearmint, *Eucalyptus radiata,* anise, ginger, lavender, marjoram, Roman chamomile, tarragon; GI Purity. M, R

Food Poisoning

Tarragon, patchouli, rosemary, thyme, *Melaleuca alternifolia.*

Foot Problems

Athlete's Foot

Melaleuca alternifolia, *Melaleuca quienquenervia*, blue cypress, lemongrass, white fir, lavender, peppermint, manuka.

Blisters

Melaleuca alternifolia; Lavender and Roman chamomile.

Corns

Lemon, tangerine, grapefruit, oregano, Myrrh, *Melaleuca alternifolia.*

Sore Feet

Peppermint, white fir, lavender, patchouli, myrrh, frankincense, sandalwood, vetiver; Trauma, Lavender and frankincense.

Frigidity

Jasmine, clary sage, rose, sandalwood, ylang-ylang; To Be Loved, Trauma.

Fungal Infections (Yeast)

Systemic Infections

Melaleuca alternifolia, white fir, blue cypress, lavender, lemongrass, rosemary, geranium, palmarosa and rosewood.

Ringworm

Melaleuca alternifolia, *Melaleuca quienquernervia*, lavender, rosemary, geranium, rosewood and myrrh.

Thrush

Cinnamon, clove, peppermint, rosemary, geranium, rosewood, orange, lavender, myrrh, *Melaleuca alternifolia.*

Vaginal Yeast

Lavender, manuka, *Melaleuca alternifolia*, rosemary, Roman chamomile, geranium, rosewood, peppermint, spearmint, mountain savory, thyme or *Laurus nobilis*.

Gallbladder/Gallstones

Geranium, ledum, carrot seed, celery, Juniper berries, Roman chamomile and German chamomile; GI Purity.

Gallstones

Lemon, orange, grapefruit, mandarin, tangerine.

Gangrene

Oregano, lavender, mountain savory, thyme, ravensara, cistus, cinnamon, *Eucalyptus globulus*, yuzu, *Melaleuca alternifolia*; Oregano and lavender.	A, C G, DS DDIL

Gastritis

Tarragon, peppermint, lavender, tea tree, Fennel, *Melaleuca alternifolia*; GI Purity.	R, M B

Gingivitis (Pyorrhea)

Tea tree, peppermint, oregano, myrrh, *Melaleuca alternifolia*.	GR MW

Gout

Juniper, geranium, helichrysum, thyme, ledum, carrot seed, celery, rosemary, Roman chamomile, lemon, *Melaleuca alternifolia*, nutmeg, peppermint; Trauma.	M, R FB B

Grazes
(abrasions)

Bergamot, German chamomile, lavender, manuka, tea tree.	W, S N, G DS

Gum Disease

Manuka, myrrh, peppermint, thyme, tea tree, *Melaleuca alternifolia*.	MW GR

Hair and Scalp

Rosemary, lavender, clary sage, sage, fennel, cedarwood, juniper, ylang-ylang, sandalwood, lemon, Roman chamomile, German chamomile, cypress, rose, rosewood, geranium, patchouli.

Gray Hair

Sandalwood oil rinse

Dandruff

Melaleuca alternifolia, rosemary, cedarwood, cypress; Shaman's Blend.

Hair loss (Alopecia)

Lavender, rosemary, ylang-ylang, sage, cedarwood, sandalwood, clary sage.

Hallitosis (Bad Breath)

Nutmeg, peppermint, tarragon.

Hangover

Cypress, fennel, grapefruit, juniper,	I,B
pine, rose, rosemary.	M, R

Head Lice

Eucalyptus radiata, lavender, blue cypress, peppermint, thyme, geranium, *Melaleuca alternifolia.*

Headache

Basil, *Eucalyptus globulus*, *E. radiata*,	I,M
grapefruit, lavender, marjoram, melissa,	R,B
peppermint, rose, rosemary. Roman chamomile, peppermint, spearmint, bergamot, lemon; Awareness.	

Stress

German chamomile, Roman chamomile, peppermint, lavender.

Migraine (Juvenile)

German chamomile, grapefruit, peppermint, rosemary.

Hormone cycle

Lavender, clary sage, anise seed, ylang-ylang, sage, fennel, bergamot, geranium.

Hypoglycemic Migraine

Peppermint, lavender, fennel, dill, coriander, lemongrass, clove, caraway, thyme, geranium.

Migraine

Helichrysum, clove, rosemary, basil, peppermint, melissa, lavender, ylang-ylang, German chamomile, *Eucalyptus radiata*, marjoram; Trauma.

Muscle Spasm

Marjoram, valerian, Blue cypress, lavender, rosemary, peppermint, lemongrass, basil, cardamom; Trauma.

Sinus

Rosemary, bergamot, *Melaleuca ericifolia*, *Eucalyptus radiata*, lavender, lemon, Geranium; Breath of Life.

Bone/Structure

Lavender, wintergreen/birch, basil, marjoram, lemongrass, rosemary; Trauma.

Hearing Loss*

Helichrysum, juniper, peppermint, geranium.

Tinitis (Ringing in ears)

Helichrysum, juniper berry, geranium, peppermint, lavender, basil.

---

* External Topical Application Around Ear

Heart Problems (Chronic)

Clove, goldenrod, lavender, Roman chamomile, helichrysum, rose, ylang-ylang; To Be Loved, Trauma, Robe of LIght.

Angina

Ginger, goldenrod, marjoram.

False angina

Orange, melissa.

Arrhythmia

Ylang-ylang, marjoram.

Tachycardia (Rapid heart beat)

Goldenrod, lavender, ylang-ylang; To Be at Peace.

Bradycardia (Slow heart beat)

Goldenrod, anise seed, mandarin, rosemary, peppermint, thyme.

Heart Attack

Solidago canadensis, helichrysum, lavender, peppermint, lemon and cypress.

Heartburn

Peppermint, lemon, spearmint, German chamomile, *Litsea cubeba*, marjoram, clove. M, R

Heat Stroke

Helichrysum, cypress, sandalwood and peppermint, *Eucalyptus radiata.*

Hematoma (Bruise)

Cypress, helichrysum, lemon, grapefruit, Clove; Trauma.

Hemorrhaging (Bleeding)

Helichrysum, geranium, rose, cistus, cypress.

Hemorrhoids

Cypress with helichrysum, spikenard, wintergreen/birch, patchouli, myrrh, myrtle, clary sage, frankincense, geranium, marjoram, rosemary, rose. A, R B, CB, SB LC

Hepatitis

Melaleuca alternifolia, *Eucalyptus globulus.*

Hernia (Hiatal)

Peppermint, lavender, lemongrass, helichrysum.

Herpes

Cold sores

Bergamot, geranium, melissa. A,N B, CB

Shingles

Bergamot, *Eucalyptus radiata*, geranium, lavender, melissa, ravensara. A, N B, CB

Hiccups

Cypress, tarragon and peppermint.

Hives

Peppermint, patchouli, Roman chamomile, lavender.

Hormone Imbalance (Menapause)

Geranium, clary sage, fennel, jasmine, rose; To Be Loved.

Hot Flashes

Geranium.

Hyperactivity

St. John's wort oil, Douglas fir, lavender, cedarwood, vetiver, Roman chamomile, peppermint, valerian; To Be at Peace.

Hyperpnoea (Rapid breathing)

Ylang-ylang, sandalwood.

Hypertension

Goldenrod, lavender, marjoram, Roman Chamomile; To Be at Peace.

Hypoglycemia

Lavender, cinnamon, cumin, clove, caraway, thyme, lemongrass, geranium, coriander, *Lippin citriodora*, dill, rosemary, ravensara.

Immune Deficiency Syndrome

Cistus, geranium, lavender, manuka, lemon, melissa, rose, rosemary, ravensara, tea tree, thyme, *Melaleuca alternifolia*, *Eucalyptus radiata*; 1st Defense, To Be Well.	B, M R, I RF

Impetigo

Lavender, manuka, tea tree, thyme, ravensara, *Melaleuca alternifolia*, *Eucalyptus radiata.*	B, R

Impotence

Ylang-ylang, clary sage, sandalwood, clove, frankincense, myrrh, ginger, nutmeg, rose, jasmine, cardamom, vetiver, black pepper; Trauma, To Be Loved.	M, B R, F

Indigestion

Cardamom, fennel, coriander, ginger, lemon, peppermint, dill, clove, spearmint; GI Purity.	M, R C

Infection (Bacterial and Viral)

Hyssop, mountain savory, cypress, rosemary, rose, lavender, lemongrass, basil, thyme, oregano, nutmeg, rosewood, frankincense, myrrh, cistus, *Melaleuca alternifolia*, sage, *Eucalyptus radiata*, *E. globulus*, bergamot, marjoram, black pepper, cinnamon, juniper, lemon, manuka, pine, ravensara, tea tree, yuzu.	A, M R, C B, G W, DS

Strep Throat

Cistrus hystrix, mountain savory, cinnamon,

lavender, Roman chamomile, German chamomile, hyssop, myrrh, myrtle, nutmeg, *Melaleuca alternifolia*, *Eucalyptus radiata*.

Whooping Cough

Cypress, rosemary, rose, lavender, lemongrass, basil, thyme, oregano, myrtle, nutmeg.

Infertility

Geranium, clary sage, rose, fennel; To Be Loved.

Inflammation

Wintergreen/birch, helichrysum, frankincense, hyssop, myrrh, marjoram, ravensara, lavender, oregano, Roman chamomile, cypress, peppermint, spearmint, spruce, German chamomile. A, B R, C G, DS

Insect Bites

Lavender, *Eucalyptus globulus*, citronella, *Melaleuca alternifolia*, peppermint, rosemary.

Insect Repellent

Peppermint, *Eucalyptus radiata*, *E. citriodora*, lemon, lime, lavender, *Melaleuca alternifolia*, cedarwood, geranium, rosemary, patchouli, citronella, sandalwood, lemongrass, thyme. RF

Insomnia

Lavender, cedarwood, German chamomile, Roman chamomile, orange, St. John's wort oil, *Rosemary verbenon*, clary sage, neroli, marjoram, sandalwood, petitgrain, ylang-ylang; To Be at Peace. B M R RF

Bowel Toxicity

St. John's wort oil, melissa, frankincense, lemon thyme, *Melaleuca alternifolia*; GI Purity.

Depression

St. John's wort, melissa, frankincense, lemon, lavender, neroli, ylang-ylang, mandarine.

Hypothyroidism (Low thyroid)

Allium sativum, myrrh, myrtle.

Influenza (Colds and Flu)

Eucalyptus globulus, *E. radiata*, cedarwood, pine; Breath of Life, 1st Defense, To Be Well, Lavender and frankincense.

Irritable Bowel Syndrome

Peppermint, anise seed, fennel, Dill, clove; GI Purity.

Itching

Lavender, Roman chamomile, *Melaleuca alternifolia.*

Jaundice

Ledum, *Amyris basalmifera*, carrot seed, Roman chamomile, German chamomile, geranium, rosemary, lemon, helichrysum.

Jet Lag

Basil, geranium, grapefruit, juniper, peppermint, Rosemary. B, M R, I RF

Joint Stiffness

Swollen

Spruce, Douglas fir, white fir, elemi, basil, rosemary, oregano, fir, wintergreen/birch, vetiver, helichrysum, *Litsea cubeba*, Roman chamomile, juniper berries, lavender, fennel; Trauma.	B, M R, C

Pain

Basil, black pepper, cedarwood, Roman or German chamomile, ginger, helichrysum, lavender, rosemary, thyme; Trauma.	B, M, R, C

Strain/sprain

Bay, black pepper, cedarwood, clary sage, ginger, helichrysum, lavender, rosemary; Trauma.	B, M R, C

Kidney Disease

Reduced Kidney Function

Juniper berry.

Kidney Stones

Wintergreen/birch, geranium, juniper berry, *Eucalyptus radiata.*

Diuretic

Ledum, rosemary, tangerine, clove, juniper berry, fennel, *Eucalyptus radiata*, grapefruit, geranium, sage.

Edema

Ledum, German chamomile, nutmeg, tangerine, cypress, orange.

Kidney Infection

Myrrh, cypress, juniper berry, sandalwood, *Melaleuca alternifolia*; 1st Defense.

Knee Cartilage Deterioration or Injury

Peppermint, white fir, Douglas fir, wintergreen/birch; Trauma.

Laryngitis

Bergamot, cypress, geranium, lavender, lemon, thyme. GR, MW

Loss of voice

Geranium, grapefruit, lemon. GR MW

Tickly throat

Clove, grapefruit, lemon. GR MW

Leg Ulcers

Melaleuca alternifolia.

Lice

Body & Head

Lavender, manuka, tea tree. B, M R, W N

Ligaments

Black pepper, lemongrass, rosemary. M, R, C

Liver and Gall Bladder Disease

Ledum, *Citrus hystrix*, achillea, *Apium Graveolen*, helichrysum, mandarin, cardamom, geranium, Roman chamomile, cypress, fennel, grapefruit, mandarin, peppermint, rosemary, juniper, thyme, lemon, carrot seed, celery, ravensara, *Melaleuca alternifolia.* C, B M, R

Liver Spots

Lemon.

Lou Gehrig's Disease (ALS)

1st Defense.

Lumbago (Low Back Pain)

Peppermint, juniper berries, oregano; Trauma.

Lupus

Cypress, lemongrass, ravensara, frankincense; 1st Defense.

Lyme Disease

Melaleuca quienquenervia, blue cypress, sandalwood, ravensara, *Eucalyptus radiata*; 1st Defense, To Be Well, Oregano and lavender.

Lymphatic System

Ledum, sandalwood, *Amyris basalmifera*, M, R
helichrysum, myrtle, lemon, grapefruit, B
lemongrass, rosemary, lavender, rose, fennel, geranium, juniper berries, manuka, ravensara, bay, yuzu.

Malaria

Lemon, thyme, *Laurus nobilis, Melaleuca alternifolia*; 1st Defense, To Be Well.

M.C.T. (Mixed Connective Tissue Disease)

Rosemary, nutmeg, lemongrass, marjoram,

peppermint, clove; Trauma.

Measles

Lavender, Roman chamomile, *Melaleuca alternifolia*, German chamomile, bergamot, German chamomile, *Eucalyptus citriodora*, *E. radiata*, geranium, manuka, ravensara, tea tree, thyme; 1st Defense, To Be Well.	A, C B, R I

Memory

Rosemary, basil, peppermint; Awareness.	I, RF

Menopause and PMS (Premenstrual Syndrome)

Clary sage, sage, anise seed, fennel, basil, bergamot, rosemary, rose, neroli, ylang-ylang, peppermint, tarragon, spikenard, marjoram, Roman chamomile, cypress, geranium, jasmine, lavender, sandalwood, vitex; To Be Loved.	B, M R, S RF

Hormone Imbalance

Geranium, rose, clary sage.

Hot Flashes

Roman chamomile, clary sage, *Eucalyptus radiata*, fennel, geranium, lavender, yuzu.

Night Sweats

Clary sage, cypress.

Endometriosis

Fennel and clary sage.

Dysmenorrhea

Clary sage, rosemary, basil, sage, marjoram,

lavender, Roman chamomile, cypress, tarragon, fennel, geranium, rose, bay, clove, peppermint, vitex.

Breast tenderness

Roman chamomile, lavender, geranium, marjoram.

Mental Fatigue

Pepper, peppermint, rosemary, basil, spearmint, pine; Awareness.

Mold Infestation

Cedarwood, lemongrass, *Melaleuca alternifolia*, lemon, thyme, oregano, *Eucalyptus globulus*; Deep Cleanser.

Morning Sickness

Peppermint, patchouli, spearmint, ginger.

Motion Sickness

Patchouli, lavender, peppermint, ginger, juniper berries, rosemary, tarragon and spearmint.

Mouth infections

Geranium, manuka, myrrh, tea tree. MW, M

Mouth Ulcers

Lemon, manuka, myrrh, tea tree. CB

Mucus Congestion

Eucalyptus radiata, *E. globulus*, *E. citriodora*, frankincense, ledum, goldenrod, M, R B, I lavender, hyssop, helichrysum, fennel, cypress, German chamomile, marjoram, mugwort, myrtle, black pepper, patchouli, rosemary, thyme, peppermint, ravensara, sage, pine, niaouli. RF

Multiple Sclerosis (MS)

Ravensara, *Eucalyptus citriodora,* rosemary, helichrysum; 1st Defense, To Be Well, Trauma.

Mumps

Thyme, thymol, manuka, lavender, melissa, myrrh, blue cypress and wintergreen/birch, German chamomile, helichrysum, *Litsea cubeba,* tea tree, *Melaleuca alternifolia*; 1st Defense, To Be Well. M, R C

Muscle Cramps and Pain

Clove, myrrh, Roman chamomile, rosemary, basil, clary sage, marjoram, elemi, bay, German chamomile, helichrysum, peppermint, ravensara, cypress, black pepper, *Eucalyptus globulus,* ginger, thyme, vetiver, lavender; Trauma. M, R B

Debility

Basil, ginger, juniper berries, lavender, marjoram, thyme. M, R B

Fatigue

Bay, black pepper, clary sage, ginger, grapefruit, juniper berries, lavender, lemongrass, pine. M, R B

Numbness

Black pepper, cinnamon, clove, geranium, ginger, helichrysum, marjoram.

Spasm

Basil, bergamot, cardamom, Roman chamomile, clary sage, clove, coriander, cypress, fennel, geranium, helichrysum, jasmine, lavender, marjoram, peppermint, petitgrain, rosemary, thyme, vetiver. M, R B, C

Muscular Dystrophy

Pine, lavender, marjoram, lemongrass, ginger, rosemary, *Eucalyptus radiata*, thyme;
Lavender and frankincense.

Nails (Brittle or Weak)

Frankincense, myrrh, lemon.

Nail Fungus

Tea tree, tagetes, melissa, manuka. R, CB

Narcolepsy

Peppermint; Awareness.

Nausea

Nutmeg, peppermint, patchouli, clove, fennel, melissa, sandalwood, ginger; GI Purify. I, M, R, RF

Neck (Stiff)

Basil, clary sage, ginger, lavender, peppermint, rosemary. B, M R

Nervous Fatigue

Achillea ligustica, juniper berries, geranium, goldenrod, helichrysum; To Be at Peace, Shaman's Blend.

Nerve Disorders

Peppermint, lavender, cedarwood, basil, clary sage, sage, rosemary, spruce, tangerine, sandalwood, *Melaleuca alternifolia*, ravensara, marjoram, palmarosa, thyme, lemongrass, wintergreen/birch, cypress and helichrysum.

Bell's Palsy

Peppermint, helichrysum, ravensara, juniper berries, thyme.

Carpal Tunnel Syndrome

Peppermint, basil, helichrysum; Trauma.

Neuritis and Neuralgia

Marjoram, helichrysum, juniper, geranium, B, M
Laurus nobilis, nutmeg, peppermint, bay, black R, C
pepper, Roman chamomile, German chamomile, clary sage, *Eucalyptus radiata*, yuzu, spearmint, lavender; Lavendar and frankincense.

Neuropathy

Peppermint, *Achillea ligustica*, solidago, helichrysum, lavender, cypress, Roman chamomile; Awareness, Lavender and frankincense.

Neurological Diseases

ALS (Lou Gehrig's Disease)

Frankincense, helichrysum, oregano, sage, juniper berries, rosemary, clove, cardamom, vitex; Trauma.

Alzheimer's Disease

Ylang-ylang, Roman chamomile, vanilla, peppermint; Awareness, Lavender and frankincense.

Huntington's Chorea
Peppermint, juniper berries, basil.

Multiple Sclerosis (MS)
Juniper berries, basil, helichrysum, geranium, peppermint, thyme, oregano, wintergreen/birch, cypress, marjoram, rosemary; Trauma.

Parkinson's Disease
Juniper berries, peppermint, vitex, ravensara.

Night Sweats

Sage, clary sage, blue yarrow, geranium.

Nose Disease

Nosebleeds
Helichrysum, cypress, frankincense, lemon, geranium, lavender. C

Dry nose
Lavender, lemon, peppermint.

Loss of the sense of smell (chronic nasal stuffiness)
Basil, peppermint, goldenrod, frankincense; Breath of Life.

Nasal polyps
Citronella, *Eucalyptus citriodora.*

Obesity

Eucalyptus radiata, fennel, juniper berries, lemon, *Litsea cubeba*, oregano, ravensara, rosemary, thyme, yuzu. B, M, R

Osteoporosis (Loss of bone density)

Wintergreen/birch

Otitis Media

Peppermint, *Melaleuca alternifolia.*

Ovarian and Uterine Cysts

Frankincense, geranium, *Melaleuca alternifolia*, oregano or cypress.

Overindulgence

Juniper, grapefruit, lemon, orange, rosemary, vetiver. — I, R, B, C, RF

Alcohol

Fennel, grapefruit, juniper, lemon, rosemary, peppermint, yuzu. — I, R M, B, C

Overweight

Fennel, grapefruit, juniper, lemon, patchouli, petitgrain, yuzu. — B, M R

Overwork

Clary sage, jasmine, lavender, *Litsea cubeba*, neroli, rosemary, ylang-ylang, yuzu. — B, M, R, RF

Pain

Chronic Pain

Peppermint, helichrysum, spruce, wintergreen/ birch, basil, cypress, ginger, clove, elemi, oregano, Douglas fir, white fir, rosemary, valerian; Trauma.

Bone and joint pain

Wintergreen/birch, cypress, fir, spruce, pine, peppermint, helichrysum; Trauma.

Muscle pain

Basil, peppermint, rosemary, verbenon, marjoram, *Eucalyptus radiata*; Trauma.

Muscle or nerve pain from injury

Peppermint, lavender, nutmeg, black pepper; Trauma.

Inflammation

German chamomile, basil, helichrysum, peppermint, melissa, vetiver, patchouli, spruce, geranium; Trauma, Lavender and frankincense.

Trauma and accidents

Sandalwood, geranium; Trauma.

Joint pain

Douglas fir, white fir, wintergreen/birch, cypress, fir, spruce, pine, peppermint, helichrysum, lemongrass; Trauma.

Pancreatitis

Geranium, vetiver, peppermint, mountain savory, oregano, lemon; GI Purity, 1st Defense.

Parasites (intestinal)

Tarragon, anise seed, basil, peppermint, ginger, lemongrass, nutmeg, fennel, juniper, lavender, manuka, patchouli, rosewood, tagetes, tea tree, cinnamon, clove; GI Purify, 1st Defense.

A, R, B, W, HDIL

Periodontal Disease (Osteoporosis of the face and jaw)

Gum infection (Pyorrhea)

Clove, cinnamon, peppermint, myrrh, *Melaleuca alternifolia.*

Bleeding gums

Mountain savory, clove, cistus, *Melaleuca alternifolia.*

Gingivitis

Helichrysum, rose, mountain savory, cistus, clove, myrrh, *Melaleuca alternifolia.*

Mouth ulcers

Myrrh, *Melaleuca alternifolia.*

Perspiration

Geranium, rosewood, cypress.

Phlebitis (Thrombosis)

Helichrysum, goldenrod, lavender; Trauma.

Plaque (Arteriosclerosis)

Helichrysum.

Pleurisy

Ravensara, mountain savory, thyme, rosemary, *Eucalyptus radiata*; Breath of Life.

Pneumonia (Emphysema)

Goldenrod, ledum, *Melaleuca alternifolia*, rosemary, clary sage, ravensara, niaouli, cypress, *Eucalyptus radiata*; 1st Defense, To Be Well, Breath of Life.

Cough

Cypress, *Eucalyptus polybracrea.*

Congestion and coughing

Goldenrod, ledum, cedarwood, cypress, myrtle, rosemary; Breath of Life.

Dry cough

Lemon, *Eucalyptus radiata, Melaleuca alternifolia.*

Sore Throat

Thyme, cypress, *Eucalyptus radiata*, peppermint, myrrh, *Melaleuca alternifolia*; 1st Defense, To Be Well.

Strep Throat

Eucalyptus globulus, oregano, thyme, frankincense, myrrh, mountain savory, white fir or Douglas fir; 1st Defense, To Be Well.

Polio

Lemon, ylang-ylang, frankincense, wintergreen/ birch, myrtle, cypress, myrrh, tarragon, sage; 1st Defense, To be Well.

Pregnancy (Postpartum)

Lavender, myrrh, geranium, Roman chamomile, rose, ylang-ylang; Lavender and frankincense.

Hemorrhoids (varicose veins)

Cypress

Lactation

Jasmine, fennel, geranium.

Mastitis (Infected breast)

Manuka, *Melaleuca quienquenervia, M. alternifolia,* tangerine, lavender; Lavender and frankincense.

Postpartum Depression

Vetiver, St. John's wort, cedarwood, mandarine, sandalwood, jasmine, geranium, rose; To Be Happy.

Prostate (Benign prostate hyperplasia)

Oregano, thyme, helichrysum, frankincense, myrrh, sage, juniper berries, yarrow, spruce, cypress.

Prostatitis

Rosemary, myrtle, clary sage, sage, mountain savory, fennel, bergamot, thyme, lavender, *Eucalyptus radiata*, tarragon, spruce, sandalwood, ylang-ylang, geranium, yarrow, clove, cinnamon, tsuga, peppermint, cypress; 1st Defense.

Psoriasis

Bergamot, Roman chamomile, geranium, M, R
Lavender, benzoin; Lavender and frankincense. C, G

Radiation

Melaleuca alternifolia, neroli; Lavender and frankincense.

Rashes

German and Roman chamomile, *Eucalyptus globulus*, *E. radiata*, lavender, tea tree. B, R, G, C DS

Raynaud's Disease

Helichrysum, goldenrod, clove, lemongrass, cypress, geranium, marjoram, rose. B, M, R

Restless Leg Syndrome

Oregano, basil, marjoram, lavender, cypress, Roman chamomile, peppermint; Trauma, To Be at Peace.

Rheumatic Fever

Mountain savory, peppermint, thyme, *Rosemary verbenon*, *Melaleuca alternifolia*, pepper, oregano, marjoram, ginger; Trauma.

Rheumatoid arthritis (Rheumatism)

Peppermint, wintergreen/birch, oregano, fir, pine, cypress, vetiver, mountain savory, bay, marjoram, basal, ginger, black pepper, cedarwood, German chamomile, Roman chamomile, clove, coriander, *Eucalyptus citriodora*, *E. globulus*, *E. radiata*, coriander, frankincense, helichrysum, juniper, lavender, lemon, manuka, rosemary, thyme, vetiver, spruce; Trauma. B, M, R

Rhinitis

Basil, *Eucalyptus radiata*, *Melaleuca alternifolia*, ravensara; Breath of Life, 1st Defense, To Be Well.

Rhinopharyngitis

Eucalyptus radiata, thyme, ravensara, *Melaleuca alternifolia*; Breath of Life.

Ringworm

Tea tree, clove, manuka, myrrh, patchouli, *Eucalyptus radiata,* oregano, lavender.	A, N, C, W, CB

Salmonella

Cinnamon, clove, peppermint, *Melaleuca alternifolia*; GI Purify, 1st Defense.

Scabies

Citronella, peppermint, palmarosa, lavadin, Roman chamomile, *Eucalyptus globulus,* black pepper, clove, cinnamon, lemon, ginger, manuka, myrrh, oregano, tea tree, thyme, niaouli; Lavender and frankincense.	A, C CB, W, B

Scalp (Disorders)

Cedarwood, lavender, manuka, rosemary, tea tree.	R, M

Scar Tissue

Helichrysum, lavender, hyssop, cypress, elemi, blue yarrow, rose, cistus, frankincense, myrrh, jasmine, neroli, palmarosa, petitgrain, rose, sandalwood; Lavender and frankincense.	M, R, FO

Sciatica

German and Roman chamomile, lavender, helichrysum, juniper, peppermint; Trauma.	C, M, R, N

Schizophrenia

Tarragon, peppermint, cardamom, cedarwood, vetiver, melissa, frankincense, rosemary, basil; To Be at Peace.

Scleroderma

Frankincense, Roman chamomile, lavender, patchouli, sandalwood, and myrrh.

Scoliosis

Oregano, thyme, basil, wintergreen/birch, cypress, marjoram, peppermint; Trauma.

Seasickness (motion sickness)

Ginger

Seizures

Ylang-ylang; Trauma, To Be at Peace.

Sexually Transmitted Diseases

Herpes simplex Type II

Melissa, ravensara, *Melaleuca alternifolia*, *Melaleuca quienquenervia*, blue cypress, oregano, thyme, cumin, mountain savory, clove or cinnamon.

Genital warts

Melissa, oregano, thyme, *Melaleuca alternifolia*, *Melaleuca ericifolia*, lavender.

Gonorrhea and syphilis

Oregano, melissa, thyme, mountain savory, cinnamon; Oregano and lavender.

Sexual Disfunction

Loss of libido (women)

Geranium, jasmine, ylang-ylang, clary sage, nutmeg, rose; To Be Loved.

Loss of libido (men)

Myrrh, black pepper, pine, ylang-ylang, ginger, nutmeg, rose; To Be Loved.

Excessive sexual desire (Sexual addiction)

Marjoram, lavender, St. John's wort, cypress.

Shingles (*Herpes zoster*)

Elemi, clove, oregano, mountain savory, blue cypress, sandalwood, *Melaleuca quienquenervia*, thyme, juniper, geranium peppermint, ravensara.

Shock

Basil, cardamom, helichrysum, *Melaleuca alternifolia*, frankincense, lavender, sandalwood, rosemary, peppermint; Trauma, Robe of Light, Shaman's Blend, Lavender and frankincense.

Sinusitis

Ravensara, basil, clove, myrtle, *Eucalyptus globulus*, *Eucalyptus radiata*, thyme, lavender, marjoram, peppermint, pine, rosemary, tea tree, lemon, niaouli; Breath of Life. N, M R, I

Skin Disorders

Melaleuca alternifolia, frankincense, helichrysum, peppermint, lavender, lemon, German chamomile, FO, S, C

Eucalyptus radiata, *Rosemary verbenon*, thyme, mountain savory, palmarosa, patchouli, rosewood, juniper, ravensara, Roman chamomile, jasmine, *Litsea cubeba*, lemongrass, mandarin, myrrh, neroli, orange, petitgrain, rose, sandalwood, ylang-ylang, yuzu, oregano. FT, LC, FM

Abscess

Thyme, myrrh, frankincense or wintergreen/birch; *Melaleuca alternifolia*, oregano and lavender, frankincense and lavender, 1st Defense.

Acne

Melaleuca alternifolia, geranium, vetiver, blue cypress, lavender, patchouli, German chamomile, Roman chamomile, rosewood, lemon, cedarwood, *Eucalyptus radiata*, orange, clove; Oregano and lavender.

Burns

Lavender, lemon; Oregano and lavender.

Chapped, dry and cracked

Roman chamomile, neroli, rose, cedarwood, vetiver, palmarosa, patchouli, sandalwood, jasmine, lavender, spikenard or myrrh.

Clogged pores (Blackheads)

Lemon, orange, *Melaleuca alternifolia*, blue cypress, geranium, patchouli; Oregano and lavender.

Diaper rash

Lavender, helichrysum, patchouli, cypress, *Melaleuca alternifolia*.

Dry (Cracked)

Chamomile, geranium, jasmine, neroli, patchouli, rose, sandalwood.

Eczema

Roman chamomile; Rose and geranium, Lavender and frankincense, palmarosa, sandalwood and patchouli.

Freckles

Lemon

Fungal infection

Oregano, lemongrass, *Melaleuca alternifolia*, *Melaleuca quenquenervia*, *Melaleuca ericifolia;* Oregano and lavender.

Itching

Peppermint, oregano, lavender, helichrysum, valerian, patchouli, Roman chamomile, *Melaleuca alternifolia.*

Moles

Frankincense, geranium, wintergreen/birch, lavender.

Oily

Bergamot, cypress, geranium, grapefruit, lavender, cedarwood, geranium, juniper, rosemary, sandalwood, lemon, ylang-ylang. FO, SW, FT, C, FM, LC

Poison oak

Peppermint, *Eucalyptus dives*, *Melaleuca alternifolia*, rosemary, lemon, lemongrass, thyme, basil, lavender, geranium.

Psoriasis

Roman chamomile, *Melaleuca alternifolia*, patchouli, helichrysum, rose, German chamomile, lavender.

Sagging skin (Loss of tone)

Lavender, helichrysum, patchouli or cypress.

Stretch marks

Lavender, frankincense, elemi, spikenard, geranium and myrrh.

Skin ulcers

Rosewood, clove, helichrysum, Roman chamomile, patchouli, myrrh or lavender.

Vitiligo

Vetiver, sandalwood and myrrh.

Wrinkles

Frankincense, helichrysum, cypress, rose, lavender, ylang-ylang, patchouli, sage, geranium, clary sage, rosewood, sandalwood, jasmine, neroli, palmarosa, spikenard.

Sleep Disorders

Lavender, valerian, goldenrod, marjoram, Roman chamomile and orange.

Smoking Cessation

Cinnamon, clove and nutmeg.

Snoring

Thyme

Sores

Roman chamomile, lavender, patchouli, blue cypress, *Eucalyptus citriodora*, vetiver, manuka, myrrh, tea tree, yuzu. A, C, CB, G, DS

Sore Throat

Melaleuca alternifolia

Spinal Pain

Wintergreen/birch, Douglas fir, spruce, peppermint, marjoram and basil.

Back ache
Clary sage, lavender, chamomile, basil, peppermint, geranium or elemi.

Bone spurs (Calcium deposits)
Geranium, rosemary, *Eucalyptus radiata*, ravensara, oregano, vetiver or elemi.

Herniated disk (Degenerative)
Helichrysum, pine, *Basil eugenol*, thyme, melissa, lemongrass; Trauma.

Lumbago (Low back pain)
Marjoram, nutmeg, basil, Roman chamomile, elemi, peppermint; Trauma.

Neck pain and stiffness
Basil, marjoram, lavender, helichrysum, wintergreen/birch, Douglas fir, white fir, nutmeg, pine, spruce, elemi, cypress, basil, peppermint; Trauma.

Sciatica

Pine, helichrysum, peppermint, nutmeg; Trauma.

Sprain

Lemon, wintergreen/birch, rose, basil, pine, spruce, cypress, peppermint, lavender, *Eucalyptus citriodora*; Trauma.

Stress

Lavender, chamomile, marjoram, rose, sandalwood, frankincense, cedarwood, *Tannecetum annum*; To Be at Peace.

Stroke

Helichrysum, cypress; Trauma.

Sunburn

Roman chamomile, *Eucalyptus radiata*, lavender. B, C N

Tachycardia

Lavender, Roman chamomile, ylang-ylang; To Be at Peace.

Tendonitis

Peppermint, spearmint, oregano, clove; Trauma.

Testicular Function (Maintain)

Rosemary, clary sage, fennel, bergamot, sandalwood, ylang-ylang, geranium, yarrow, pine.

Thrush (Candidiasis)

Melaleuca alternifolia

Thyroid

Hyperthyroid (Grave's disease)
Myrrh, spruce, blue tansy, lemongrass.

Hypothyroid
Ledum, lemongrass, myrtle, peppermint, spearmint, myrrh, clove.

Tinnitis (Ringing in ears)

Peppermint; Trauma (not to be placed in ear).

Tiredness

Basil, grapefruit, lemon, peppermint, rosemary, yuzu. — I, B, RF, M

Tonic (General)

Cedarwood, Roman chamomile, *Eucalyptus citriodora*, frankincense, helichrysum, lemon, lemongrass, *Litsea cubeba*, melissa, orange, ravensara, rose, rosemary, yuzu. — M, R, B

Tonsillitis

Clove, goldenrod, oregano, mountain savory, ravensara, Roman chamomile, lavender, manuka, tea tree, yuzu, thyme, *Melaleuca alternifolia*; 1st Defense, To Be Well. — MW, G, R

Toothache

Clove, wintergreen/birch, German chamomile, Roman chamomile, *Melaleuca alternifolia*, oregano, peppermint. — C, M, MW, CB

Toxemia

Fennel, tangerine, orange, cypress, lemon; To Be Well.

Trauma (Emotional)

Bergamot, Roman chamomile, lavender, rose, yuzu, jasmine, neroli, geranium, ylang-ylang; Trauma, To Be Loved.

Tuberculosis

Ravensara, *Rosemary verbenon*, lemon, cinnamon, sandalwood, *Eucalyptus spp.*, lavender; Breath of Life, 1st Defense, To Be Well, Deep cleanser (for environment).

Tumors

Frankincense.

Typhoid Fever

Ravensara, cinnamon, peppermint, black pepper, mountain savory; 1st Defense.

Ulcerations

German chamomile, *Eucalyptus globulus*, *E. radiata*, geranium, juniper, lavender, myrrh, tea tree. A, C, G, W S, DS, CB

Ulcers (Stomach)

Clove, cinnamon, rose, oregano, thyme.

Urinary Tract (Bladder infection)

Oregano, mountain savory, sage, fennel, rosemary, lavender, sandalwood, hyssop, *Melaleuca alternifolia*.

Vaginal Infection

Myrrh, mountain savory, oregano, *Melaleuca alternifolia*, thyme linalol.

Varicose veins (Spider veins)

Helichrysum, basil, cypress, wintergreen/birch, peppermint, lemongrass, lavender, tangerine, bergamot, geranium, juniper berries or lemon.	A, B R, C

Vascular Cleansing

Helichrysum, cypress, frankincense, German chamomile, Roman chamomile, lemongrass, geranium or cardamom.

Warts (Genital)

Thyme linalol, *Melaleuca alternifolia*, frankincense, hyssop, clove, lemon, manuka, tea tree.	A, N C, CB

Wounds (Scrapes, Cuts)

Melaleuca quienquenervia, thyme, clove, oregano, rosemary, *Melaleuca alternifolia,* bergamot, Roman chamomile, *Eucalyptus citriodora*, frankincense, lavender, manuka, myrrh, tea tee; Oregano and lavender.	W, N C, S

Worms

Cinnamon, clove; 1st Defense.

Wrinkles

Frankincense, sandalwood, rose, geranium, cypress, lemongrass, palmarosa; Lavender and frankincense.

Yeast Infection

Candidiasis (systemic)

Manuka, melissa, *Melaleuca alternifolia.*	S, B M, B R

Thrush

Manuka, melissa, *Melaleuca alternifolia.*	MW, GR

The use of essential oils for the purposes of self medication and as home remedies goes back to the days of ancient China and Egypt some 4,500 to 6,000 years ago.

Humanity's long experience with the use of essential oils has seen a widespread international resurgence in their use in the 20th and 21st centuries; and it is not unusual for these essential oils to be found in the medicine cabinet of the poor, middle class and wealthy households.

It is each individual's responsibility to learn when essential oils can be used as an exclusive therapy for a particular health problem or as part of a more complex therapy program using nutritional supplements and/or other OTC or prescription therapeutic agents.

Bibliography

Anon: Essential Oils: Desk Reference. Second Ed. Essential Science Publishing. USA. 2002

Aqel, M.B.: Relaxant effect of the volatile oil of Rosmarinus officinalis on tracheal smooth muscle. J Ethnopharmacol. 1991: 33 (1-2). 57- 62.

Aruna, K. and Sivaramakrishnan, V.M.: Anticarcinogenic Effects of the Essential Oils from Cumin, Poppy and Basil. Food Chem. Toxicol. 1992:30 (11). 953-956.

Bassett, I.B., et al: A comparative study of tea-tree oil versus benzoylperoxide in the treatment of acne. Med J Aust. 1990:153 (8). 455-8.

Benencia, F. et al.: Antiviral activity of sandalwood oil against herpes simplex viruses-1 and 2. Phytomedicine. 1999:6 (2). 119-23.

Carson, C.F. et al.: Antimicrobial activity of the major components of the essential oil of Melaleuca alternifolia. J Appl Bacterriol. 1995:78(3). 264-269.

Dolara, P. et al: Analgesic effects of myrrh. Nature. 1996. Jan 4: 379(6560).29.

Edwards, V.: The Aromatherapy Companion. Storey Books. North Adams, MA. 1999.

Fischer-Rizzi, S.: Complete Aromatherapy Handbook. Sterling Publishing Co., Inc. New York. 1990.

Gattefosse', Rene'-Maurice. Aromatherapy. Saffron Walden. UK. C.W. Daniel & Co. 1993.

Guenther, Ernest. The Essential Oils. Malabar. Florida.1950.

Halioua, B and Ziskind, B.: Medicine in the Days of the Pharaohs. The Belknap Press of Harvard University Press. Cambridge, Massachusetts and London, England. 2005.

Keville, K.: Aromatherapy for Dummies. IDG Books Worldwide, Inc. Dummies Press. Indianapolis. 1999.

Keville, K. and Green, M.: Aromatherapy. The Crossing Press. Freedom, CA. 1995.

McGlivery, C. and Reed, J.: Essential Aromatherapy. Acropolis Books, Enderby, England. 1993.

McGuffin, M. et al: Botanical Safety Handbook, CRC Press. Boca Raton, FL. 1997.

Niazi, H.: The Egyptian Prescription. Cairo, Egypt. Elias Modern Press. 1988.

Penoel, Daniel. Natural Home Health Care Using Essential Oils. . Essential Science Publishing. Salem, UT. 1998.

Ryman, D.: Aromatherapy: The Complete Guide to Plant and Flower Essences for Health and Beauty. New York. Bantam Books. 1993.

Tisserand, R. and Balacs, T. (Ed.): Essential Oil Safety. Churchill Livingston. New York. 1995.

Valnet, J. and Tisserand, R. (ed): The Practice of Aromatherapy. Healing Arts Press. Rochester, VT. 1990.

Wallach, J.D. and Ma, L.: Let's Play Doctor. Wellness Publications, LLC. 1989.

Wallach, J.D. and Ma, L.: Let's Play Herbal Doctor. Wellness Publications, LLC. 2000.

Wallach, J.D. and Ma, L.: Rare Earths: forbidden cures. Wellness Publications, LLC. 1994.

Wallach, J.D. and Ma, L.: Dead Doctors Don't Lie. Wellness Publications, LLC. 1998.

Wallach, J. D. and Ma, L.: God Bless America. Wellness Publications, LLC. 2001.

Wallach, J.D. and Ma, L.: Hell's Kitchen. Wellness Publications, LLC. 2005.

Wildwood, C.: The Bloomsbury Encyclopedia of Aromatherapy. Bloomsbury Publishing Plc. London. 1996.

Worwood, V. A.: The Complete Book of Essential Oils and Aromatherapy. New World Library. Novato, CA. 1991.

Worwood, S. and Worwood, V.A.: essential aromatherapy. New World Library. Novato, California. 2003.

Index

A

B

C

D

E

F

G

H

I

J

K

L

M

N

O

P

Q

R

S

T

U

V

W

Y

Z